Crushed

A Journey Through Depression

By Linda Bjork

© 2017

ISBN 978-0692047484

Manuscript design by Aubrey Bjork
Cover Design by Melanie Jensen
© 2017

To my family.

This book, and my life, are dedicated to you.
I love you more than words can express.
Thank you for your patience with me.

CONTENTS

WHAT READERS ARE SAYING

Wow!!! I have many thoughts and feelings as I read this… I have much to ponder. You are incredibly amazing and I'm so impressed with how you have put together this awesome book and shared your inner self that you spent so much time stuffing and hiding… I can't get it out of my mind… Thanks so much for writing this. It is awesome.

- Jennifer S.

Oh wow, Linda what a book… Thank you, this a book that will help everyone who reads it… I must say it is a page turner… So when does this book go on sale? Soon I hope.   I know someone who really needs it. I am so proud of you for doing this.

- Marie R.

I just finished your wonderful book… Your amazing gift with the written word is a delight to read… I came away better knowing you, and frankly, better knowing myself… Reading this has helped me notice ways in which I might be following a path of brokenness. Our stories may be different but there was a surprisingly similar reaction to the circumstances… I am forever grateful for the healing you are seeking for your difficult road traveled. It is inspirational to me. Thank you for sharing it.

- McKenna N.

Your email came just in the right time and you sharing your most personal thoughts with me was what I needed at this time in my life… I thought I was doing quite well until I read what you wrote.

In the last year I decided I will no longer let anyone or anything hurt me. I don't give a damn about what anyone says or thinks of me, and I most definitely will never allow myself to feel hurt, defeat, sorrow, happiness, excitement or be emotional in any way or form. I was ICE and nothing will ever touch me again. I was numb. Emotions were a sign of being weak and I'm not weak. I'm solid like ice and colder than ice... as I read, it's like I was transported back in time... all the emotions came flooding back and I wasn't just reading about it I was physically & emotionally in it. This ice princess melted faster than real ice...lol... I cried for the first time in a year... you have again pulled me out of the abyss of darkness... After reading what you wrote my mind started to search within myself and some of the things I found are not pleasant but I feel a little bit of relief. I know I still have a lot more to dig into. Your experiences and the steps you are taking to find resolutions are a tremendous help to me... It's time to melt the rest of this ice off of me. I'm actually smiling while I'm typing those words...and crying you a river at the same time...

- Ofa F.

I just opened it up and read the first few pages and look forward to reading the rest. I'm going to need a big box of tissues.

- Connie S.

FOREWORD

Your 'mess' is your message.

I can't count the number of times that phrase has run through my mind in all my trainings with 3 Key Elements, not to mention all the times I've said it to myself, those I coach and present to, and my personal mentoring clients.

Our life is such a personal journey, sacred and meaningful to our very soul. Yet we do not travel alone. We cross paths with so many, walking alongside some for lengthy periods of time. When our journey is smooth, we blindly assume it's the same for all those around us; yet when it becomes difficult, we believe we're the only one in the world who feels as we do. We hide our struggles deep inside, not wanting others to think we are 'different'. They might not accept us if they knew who we 'really' were. Surrounded by people, we feel completely alone.

If we only knew.

How often we fail to see or hear beyond the typical response of, "Fine", to our repeated question, "How are you?" That's what they all say. Everybody's fine. It's just 'you' who's not. How wrong we are when we think that way. Every person on this earth is having their own inward battles at one time or another. They may be unique, but they're oh so similar. There are always those who've gone before us on this rutty, potholed road called life, and there are always those just a few feet behind. Wouldn't it be nice to know how they made it through? Or even to have the hope that we CAN make it through a terribly difficult spot?

If we'd only be vulnerable and open our mouths and hearts to others and share what we've learned, to let them know we're not always 'fine', we could save those around us so much grief. And as we do so, they not only accept us, they feel safe with us, knowing we are just like them!

As I've worked to overcome my own inward battles, there is nothing more rewarding or more fulfilling than sharing my personal journey to help others through theirs. There are so many tools and truths we can use to be able to see life more clearly, so we can get out of our ruts and avoid the potholes before us. It has been my joy and privilege to share these truths with my own sister Linda as she took my outstretched hand and we walked side by side for a while to help get her 'out'. No sooner is she moving forward than she is reaching out to offer light to others to help them on their own personal journey.

This is so Linda—always caring, always lifting in her own unique way. She is a gifted writer and storyteller, using her talent to inspire others to find the hope she has found—hope that propelled her forward in life-changing ways. There is always hope, if we can only open up to have faith in ourselves, those around us, and in our God who loves us so much. As we do, we can then become his hands—his light to help others experience life in the joyous manner he always intended for us to have.

I invite you to walk with Linda as she shares her own personal journey. As you do, you will recognize similar struggles within yourself. That is where the battle lies—in our minds and hearts with our thoughts and feelings. Learn how she turned the tide of her own inner war and is now on the winning side, transforming her life into the one she always dreamed of, but never thought she could have.

Suzanne Lindsay
Life Unblocked

INTRODUCTION

"You have no idea how I feel!" she yelled, "You have no idea what my life has been like!"

She was absolutely right. Sort of. My friend had been raised in squalor and abuse by her undereducated mother and a string of stepfathers, all of dubious character. When my friend introduced me to her sister—well, technically her half-sister, since all her siblings were fathered by different men—she said, "This is my sister, her father was murdered, but my father wasn't the one who killed him."

I had forgotten that my friend's father had been imprisoned for murder. He wasn't a part of her life and she didn't talk about him. My friend had met missionaries in her youth, changed her life, and pulled herself out of the gutter to become one of the most remarkable people I've ever known. She currently teaches at a university and is a sought-after motivational speaker.

Her husband, on the other hand, grew up in a middle class home that, while not perfect, was nothing like what she had endured growing up.

On this particular day, early in their marriage, the ghosts of miseries past were haunting my friend and she was emotionally distraught. Her well-meaning husband had made the insulting and inexcusable mistake of uttering the words, "I understand how you feel."

Rather than being repulsed by her vehement rebuff, he continued earnestly, "Have you ever felt lonely?"

"Yes," she replied.

"So have I," he said. "Have you ever felt rejected?"

"Yes," she replied.

"So have I," he said. "Have you ever felt like you're not good enough?"

"Yes," she replied.

"So have I," he said. "Have you ever felt unworthy of being loved?"

"Yes," she replied.

"So have I," and he continued listing emotion after emotion until she softened and realized that although they had had vastly different experiences and although he couldn't understand what she'd been through, he might be able to understand how she felt, because he had felt that way too. It opened her eyes and her heart and allowed her husband to be a help and support to her.

Likewise, although my life experiences will be vastly different from yours, we may be alike in many ways. If you have ever felt lonely, unloved, humiliated, ashamed, anxious, depressed, worried, abandoned, betrayed, forlorn, lost, insecure, vulnerable, nervous, helpless, hopeless, discouraged, rejected, sad, angry, afraid, jealous, overwhelmed, confused, frustrated, taken for granted, insecure, unsupported, unworthy or worthless then we have something in common.

This book is a chronicle of my journey from anxiety, depression, and brokenness back to wholeness and happiness. But it isn't about me; it's about all of us who are broken and crushed. If the process works for one, it should work for all, since we're dealing with the same issues. Although I had no hope and felt doomed to a life consisting of merely existing and enduring, I'm pleased to say that I was wrong, and it's one of those times when being wrong is a really good thing.

THE BC EPOCH

I sat cross-legged on the powder blue carpet and gingerly lifted Lela's bare foot to my lap. Conversation paused briefly as I applied lotion and gently began to massage. Her eyes closed as she inhaled and exhaled slowly, her frail body leaning back against the padded rocking chair, her arms resting on the armrests and a white knitted cap covering the place where her hair had once been. This wasn't Lela's first battle with cancer, but we both knew that it would be her last. At each weekly visit, I gently massaged her hands and feet while we talked.

At that moment I was immensely grateful for Susan, another friend who had emerged victorious from her battle with breast cancer, who explained how the chemo affected her hands and feet, leaving them numb and tingly. It was through her experience that I learned that although I could not take away the reality, or the fear or the pain, I wasn't completely powerless. I could at least massage those aching hands and feet and bring some small measure of comfort and relief. I could also listen. I couldn't make it all better, but at least I could do something. Armed with those two meager tools, I visited with her regularly during her recovery. With the lessons learned, literally at Susan's feet, I was better prepared to respond when I learned of Lela's relapse.

Lela and I had visited many times over a course of many years. I had been with her as she endured bouts of unemployment, illness, surgery, etc. and Lela always amazed me. Whenever I came to lift and encourage, it was always me who left lighter. Lela had a way of making me feel special and I loved to be with her.

At this visit, she evaluated her life and measured it against a blessing she had once been given where she was assured of her tremendous influence as a mother. She was concerned about her granddaughter who lived with her and who she helped raise since the girl's mother had never married and wasn't in a good place in her life. She was concerned about her husband's future loneliness and her other grown children and the choices they were making. She laughed as she told me, "I told them I'd come back and haunt them if they don't make good choices, and I'll do it too."

"I believe you Lela," I smiled.

"What are they going to do without me?" she wondered.

"I think they're going to have to grow up and start 'adulting' since they can't rely on you to do it for them. The training wheels are coming off, and they're going to rise to the occasion. I think they'll be okay," I reassured her.

She talked about her decades of service with the Boy Scouts and how many teenage boys she had mentored over the years. I was keenly aware of her service since my own son was one of the young men that she mentored. When a Boy Scout earns the rank of Eagle, he is honored at an award ceremony and given two pins to bestow on others to symbolize that he didn't accomplish this honor on his own. One is a mother's pin and the other is a mentor's pin bestowed on a person who has been a significant influence in the young man's life. Lela had more than a dozen mentor pins displayed on a plaque on her living room wall.

"I think my most successful 'mothering' has been to other people's children," Lela said.

"You felt drawn to serve in scouting, you knew that's what you were supposed to be doing. I have no doubt that you have successfully completed your life's mission. How many people can say that they know they completed what they came here to do? You did it and did it well. I'm proud of you." I nodded.

I gently set her foot down and picked up the other one, applied lotion and began to massage.

"Thank you," she sighed and looked in my eyes. "Did you know that my favorite memory of you is the image of you standing in my garbage can?"

"Hardly complimentary," I laughed.

"Do you remember that time? I was frustrated with my overgrown yard and had exhausted myself trimming rose bushes. I had piles of branches all over the yard and felt totally overwhelmed by the amount of work left to do. Then suddenly and without warning, you appeared, work gloves in hand, and started putting the branches into the garbage can. When the can was overflowing, you climbed in and stomped them down so there was room for more. I thought, 'Why is this beautiful woman standing in my garbage can? Why would she do that for me?'" Tears flowed freely down her cheeks.

"Because you're my friend and I love you." Tears coursed down my cheeks as well. I set down her foot and stood to embrace her. It was time for me to go, "Goodbye my friend."

"Till we meet again," she replied.

That was the last time I saw Lela before she passed away. It is a cherished memory and a highlight of my life.

—

We sat side by side on the freestanding porch swing in my backyard, gently rocking back and forth, enjoying the warm sensation of the late spring sunshine. Tina's three young children played happily in the yard. The youngest came over and asked, "Can we pick the peas from the garden?"

"Go for it," I smiled. He dashed away, delighted by the new experience of searching for ripe pods to pick and the thrill of finding edible hidden treasures in each one. I waited patiently until Tina was ready to speak.

Finally she blurted out, "Okay, I think I'm ready to do it. Thanks for letting me come over. I told you on the phone that I had to tell you something." She rushed on before her courage failed. "I'm a recovering addict. I'm addicted to prescription painkillers, but I've been sober for two years now."

She cringed visibly, waiting for my response.

"Sober for two years? That's incredible! Overcoming addiction is so hard; that's an amazing success," I exulted. "I'm so proud of you!"

"Proud of me? I thought you'd be shocked to know that I'm an addict. I was afraid you wouldn't want me around. I thought you'd be disgusted with me," she continued. "I'm disgusted with myself. How could I fall this low? If you only knew the things I've done."

She looked away, "I'm a mom. I have three little kids. I know better."

"Addiction is powerful. You become a slave to it, and it seems impossible to escape slavery. Some don't even try. Many try and fail, but you've obviously been fighting and not only fighting, you've been winning. You said you've been sober for two years. I know that took tremendous effort and struggle. There's a huge story in those words 'I've been sober for two years.'" I looked into her eyes. "I'm amazed by you."

Addiction is powerful. You become a slave to it, and it seems impossible to escape slavery.

She paused before saying her next words. "I've never thought to be proud of my sobriety. I've only been ashamed by my addiction."

As her story unfolded, it seems to have started indirectly with a childhood accident. She slipped off a forty foot cliff during a family camping trip and it's a miracle that she survived. She was rescued by a Boy Scout troop who were hiking nearby and the boys' leaders carried her broken body back to her family. In retrospect, one of the foremost rules of first aid is that you should never move a person with a possible neck injury, but the adrenaline and panic of an emergency make people forget their first aid training. It's a miracle that she wasn't paralyzed. The recovery was long and slow and obviously included the use of painkillers.

Then she grew up and life happened. Her military husband was deployed leaving her alone to care for the constant needs of small children. She still deals with the ever present after-effects of that childhood injury and required another surgery. The doctors prescribed painkillers and when she took them, she noticed that not only did the physical pain decrease, but the emotional pain was numbed as well. For the first time in a long time she didn't feel completely miserable and hopeless. As the painkiller wore off and the pain of every kind returned, she longed for the escape that came in that bottle. Eventually, that escape became the most important thing in the world—more important than love for husband, responsibility to care for children, responsibility to manage a household, and relationships with parents and family. Certainly more important than honesty and integrity, and the necessary lies constructed a web that seemed impossible to untangle. Impossible to escape.

For the first time in a long time she didn't feel completely miserable and hopeless.

Even moreso for Tina than in most cases, since she could never be completely free from painkillers. She needed them, legitimately needed them, so they would always be in the house. The willpower to use them as directed and not abuse them would be a challenge her entire life.

"My husband is being deployed again, and I'm afraid that I'll slip back into former habits. I need some help and support. Can I report to you each week? Knowing that I'll be accountable will really help me."

"Of course," I replied, "come each week just like you did today and we'll sit on the swing and visit. The kids love playing here so it will be an outing for them as well. Besides," I smiled, "it has the added benefit that I'll get to see you often. That's a plus for me."

"Thank you, that means so much," she said, "Oh, there's one more thing. Will you come to my ARP meeting with me?"

"Sure. What's an ARP meeting?" I queried.

"Addiction Recovery Program," she clarified.

"Oh, of course. When and where is the meeting?" I replied.

I loved the ARP meeting.

—

She saw me first even though I had been scanning frantically through the sea of faces to find her.

"Linda," she called out.

When I heard my name, I stopped and searched until I found the source of the voice. She was seated on a molded plastic seat, and I was somewhat surprised that she didn't rush to meet me, but as I dashed toward her, she arose and we embraced.

"I'm going to have to let go soon. I'm not supposed to touch anyone. They're watching me," she whispered quickly in my ear.

Somewhat confused, I let go and backed away while she quickly sat down again. There were two men seated on either side of her, watching us intently. It took a moment for my brain to register that these were plain clothes cops who were guarding her, or perhaps guarding people from her? One spoke to me.

"Who are you and what are you doing here?"

"My name is Linda," I replied. "I am Meleofa's friend and I've come to see her and say goodbye."

"How did you know where to go? Who told you where she'd be?" he demanded. "That's classified information. No one was supposed to know."

"I didn't know where she'd be. No one told me anything. All I knew is that she was being deported today. I searched on the computer to find every possible flight route that goes to Samoa today. I made a list of possible connecting flights and I planned to wait at the gate of each one until I found her. I got an airline ticket to San Diego so I could get past security," I held up my boarding pass. "I got lucky, I've only been searching for an hour."

"You shouldn't be here," he warned.

"I'm a ticketed passenger in an international airport. I have every right to be here," I countered testily. "Look," I added in a calmer voice, "I'm no threat to you. We're in a public place. I'm not doing anything wrong. I haven't seen Meleofa in person for ten months except one time, and that was through a glass barrier where we got to speak over the phone. She's leaving today and I may never get to see her again. I want her to know that she's not alone. She needs to know that she has support and that people love her. I realize that you're only doing your job, but you don't know her. I do. I know her. She is my friend and she is wonderful."

No one can replace a wife and mother. That's just not possible.

He softened. "I can see your point."

"Well," he hesitated, "let's go sit over there where there are less people and you can talk to her."

We moved over to a section near a bank of empty chairs. I sat down next to her and she spoke quickly and quietly of the horrors of the past few days and the disappointment and anger that all of her petitions over the past ten months had been denied. We had had hopes dashed again and again as court hearing after court hearing was postponed. Then came the final devastation of the court's decision. Her ten months of incarceration led not to freedom and exoneration as we had hoped, but immediate deportation instead.

During all that time, her husband and children had dealt with the loss of wife and mother and the humiliation of the whole situation. I had done what little I could, visiting the family regularly and offering support and help as needed, but no one can replace a wife and mother. That's just not possible.

"Thanks for taking my daughter dress shopping for the prom and for going with her to get senior pictures," she said.

"Oh, that was a pleasure. She's so beautiful," a smile briefly crossed my face as I thought of her lovely daughter. Then I frowned, "but I'm so sorry that you weren't able to be the one who went with her. This whole thing is just so wrong."

"Your country has stupid immigration laws," she spat bitterly.

I nodded, noticing the way she emphasized the word "your" and feeling the betrayal in her voice that her home for decades no longer belonged to her.

I had brought a carry-on bag filled with books and treats to help distract her during the long flights ahead, but the guards wouldn't let me give it to her. I couldn't give her anything.

The guards fidgeted uncomfortably as they watched us and listened to our conversation. After a while they decided that I really shouldn't be seated next to her and asked me to move and sit in the seat directly across from her instead. I moved and sat down again. Our stolen time together was drawing to a close since it would soon be time for her to board the flight.

"My family is saving money so they can come visit me in Samoa in a few months. You could come too, if you want. You're certainly invited," she said.

I silently pondered the logistics involved. I'd never traveled to Samoa. It was so far away and would take several flights to get there. I would have to be away from my family for at least a week in order to get there, have time to visit, and return home. Could I make arrangements? Did I dare?

"Thanks for coming today," she continued. "Thanks for being here for me through all of this; I don't know how I would have made it through if I didn't have you to talk to every day."

"Every day?" I asked, bewildered. I had communicated as frequently as the law allowed: writing letters; making occasional phone calls (she could call me collect, but I couldn't call her); and even hazarding a single in-person visit through a glass wall where the sight of her in an orange jumpsuit hurt my heart. She had looked so forlorn and had lost a lot of weight. Usually I was updated on her status through her family and I spoke to them often, but not every day.

"We didn't talk every day," I said.

"No, we didn't talk every day, but I talked to you every day. I had conversations with you constantly while I sat in my cell. I told you everything. You kept me company every step of the way."

"Really? That's awesome. I've always wanted to be an imaginary friend," I teased, then added more seriously, "I'm glad I got to be there with you in some way. I'm glad that you didn't feel completely alone."

"We're now ready to begin boarding flight 2260 to Los Angeles."

The intercom announcement signaled that it was time to go. We rose from our seats and embraced. I held her tightly, holding back the tears that wanted to come. It wasn't time to cry yet; I wanted to leave her with a smile.

"Goodbye my friend. We'll keep writing and I'll be able to have a phone now," she said.

"Oh, that will make a difference. Even though you'll be farther away, we'll be able to talk more. How ironic," I mused. "Have a safe journey. I'll miss you terribly, but I will see you again.

I'm going to come to Samoa to visit you."

And I did.

—

That's the person that I used to be in my "BC" epoch; the time before I was crushed. That's the person that I hope to be able to become again. I wasn't rich or powerful or famous or glamorous, but I could stand in a garbage can, I could visit on a porch swing, and I could be an imaginary friend in a prison cell. I wasn't a saint, unless I can use the definition that a saint is a sinner who keeps on trying; I can claim that.

I missed me. I missed the me was merely broken and not completely crushed. When I was just broken, I could still function and I could still reach out and lift others. The crushed me was useless and wished to cease to exist.

Which life experience crushed me? Was it experiencing poverty to the level where I couldn't afford to buy milk and wondered how I would be able to feed my children? No, although I can't say that I enjoyed that one, my husband and I worked our way through it. We traveled through poverty, but didn't settle down and make it our permanent residence.

Was it experiencing sickness so severe that I actually broke a rib coughing? No, I didn't enjoy that one either, but the illness eventually ended and broken bones mend.

Was it the time my son was in a motorcycle accident and I arrived at the scene of the accident in time to see my son's broken body lying in the middle of an intersection surrounded by flashing lights and emergency personnel? No, although that's an image that I will never forget, we rejoice in the fact that he wasn't killed or paralyzed and his lengthy recovery was, in fact, a recovery.

Was it the hellish night where we were awoken by a phone

call that our nine month-old grandson had been life flighted to Primary Children's Hospital with hydrocephalus and required life-saving brain surgery? I'll never forget the scene of holding my daughter-in-law's hand through the night while she writhed on the floor and sobbed inconsolably, sick with bronchitis and unable to accompany her infant son to the hospital, as we awaited the expected news of his death. I felt so helpless. I couldn't help my grandson and I couldn't help my daughter-in-law. I couldn't make it all better. It was indescribably awful, but that wasn't what crushed me. Miraculously the surgery was successful and my grandson, although damaged, lived.

Which life experience crushed me? Actually, I'm not going to divulge that. The particulars don't matter anyway since our experiences are uniquely and individually tailored for each person and an experience that one person can endure might be just the thing that breaks or crushes another, like the experience that crushed my mother, and in turn led to my initial and lifelong brokenness.

BROKEN

I was born into a family of storybook perfection. My parents loved each other and were committed to making home and family a happy place. My mother's joy came from raising her children. Our lives were the center of her world. There were seven of us with a spread of eighteen years between the oldest and the youngest. I was the second to youngest.

She especially rejoiced in her close relationship with her oldest child, Becky. They were best friends. Because she loved Becky so much, it was bittersweet when a handsome young man swept her daughter off her feet and altered their relationship. My mother was prepared to rejoice with her daughter in her new love and support her in her upcoming roles as wife and eventually as a mother, but she was not prepared for her future son-in-law's version of what that future should look like.

Like most young people, he assumed that marriage meant picking up his lovely bride and transplanting her into his familiar world. In this case that meant leaving her family and moving 2,000 miles away to be near his family. Furthermore, due to a limited budget and the expense of flights and long distance phone calls, she would be able to call her parents once each month and might travel to visit her family once every two years. The young couple had no idea what the ripple effects in the wake of these decisions would be.

My mother was devastated and felt absolutely betrayed by her daughter's apparent willingness to abandon her so completely. Her world collapsed. She was heartbroken and crushed. She built emotional walls to protect herself. She had given her all and decided aloud that if that's what children do to you, then she would never get close to her children again. I was six years old.

It was like flipping off a lightswitch. My mother who had

once cuddled me and read to me suddenly would have nothing to do with me. I was still fed and clothed and basic needs were met, but the wall between us was palpable. I was shocked and confused. What had I done wrong? It must have been awful. What was wrong with me? I knew that she was a loving person, but she no longer loved me. There must have been something about me specifically that was unworthy of love.

I felt that way my whole life. There was love in the world, but not for me, because I was unlovable. As an adult and a leader of youth I have often taught the young women that I worked with that they are daughters of a Heavenly Father who loves them. As I looked around the room at the beautiful teenage girls whom I loved dearly, I felt an absolute conviction that those words applied to each and every one of them; but, deep in my heart, I felt an equally strong conviction that those words did not apply to me because I was unloveable.

I knew that some people were loved and supported, but I was not worthy of love and support.

A few seemingly insignificant life events cemented my new reality into my mind. At my elementary school we prepared a special evening program for our parents. I was now ten years old, and I already knew from experience that my parents would not come. The school was nearby, so I walked alone to perform in the program where the auditorium was filled with hundreds of people, but not one of them had come to support me, and then I walked home alone. I knew that some people were loved and supported, but I was not worthy of love and support. I tried not to expect it, tried not to be disappointed, but the hurt was deeply felt.

That pattern has continued throughout my life. I know that people won't want to come to support me, so I don't ask, and when they don't come, my reality is validated.

When I graduated from college, the auditorium was filled

with thousands of people, but not a single seat was filled with a person who had come to support me.

I have always had terrible anxiety about hosting any kind of activity or party, because I know in my heart that if I'm the host, no one will come.

I longed to be important to somebody. I longed to matter to somebody, I especially longed to matter to my family where I felt utterly invisible.

When I was twelve, I was gifted with an opportunity that I thought would solve all my problems. My grandmother invited me to fly to California with her to visit my uncle's family. This was my big chance. It was perfect. I had never flown in an airplane and had only been to the airport a handful of times in my life. Each time my sister arrived for her bi-annual visits, the whole family came to meet her at the airport and she was greeted like a rockstar. I had also been to the airport to welcome home my older brothers as they returned home from foreign missions and they were welcomed like heroes. It was a party. The whole family came and there were flowers and signs and balloons.

That had been the experience every single time I had ever been to the airport. I thought it was always like that. Airports were magical and now it was my turn. I couldn't wait for my trip with my grandmother. I didn't care about flying in an airplane or swimming in my uncle's pool or playing with my cousins—all I cared about was that magical return flight when I would, for the first time in my life, be the one arriving at the airport.

I was so excited. I could see it all in my mind. My whole family would come to pick me up and they would be happy and excited to see me. I was going to be important now, too. I was finally going to matter.

When our plane landed I was nervous, but giddy with excitement. When we emerged from the plane and saw no familiar faces among the crowds of people, I was devastated. There were no greetings, no balloons, no family members with open arms.

A few moments later, my father arrived alone to drive us home in an unfamiliar car. He had traded in our old car and bought a new one while I was away. Not only did no one come to greet me, but life had improved because of my absence.

I now knew without a doubt, that I would never be important to my family and there was absolutely nothing that I could do to change that. I resigned myself to my role of invisibility and insignificance. I resigned myself to my unalterable brokenness.

Of course, you can still live a meaningful life when you're broken. Look at the people all around you. Look to the left. Look to the right. Look into the mirror. You can get up each day and go to school or work and fulfill your responsibilities. You can laugh and love and grow and serve. You can fall in love and marry and have children. You can experience joy and pain and deal with the experiences of life and keep moving forward.

I was broken for over forty years and my life had been good. It was very good. I was used to my brokenness; it was familiar and familiarity was comfortable.

CRUSHED

Many years later, I had an experience perfectly tailored to crush me. In imagining all the things that could possibly go wrong in my life, this one was never even on the radar.

It wasn't like being hit by a semi-truck, a single powerful devastating blow; it was rather like being hit by an earthquake. Sometimes the greatest damage isn't done by the initial earthquake; it comes from the related aftershocks. The earthquake damages the foundations and the aftershocks bring down the weakened buildings.

When my personal earthquake hit, it brought me to my knees. When I tried to stand again, another aftershock knocked me down. That process repeated itself over and over until I didn't dare stand. I was metaphorically crouched in the fetal position in a corner, hiding from the next threat. The depression and anxiety were all consuming.

I went for a drive by myself, desperately longing for death to end my pain, mentally begging the cars around me to crash into me. *But please, don't just hurt me, make sure you hit me hard enough to kill me.*

I drove to a secluded place where I could sob in solitude. I did not think that I could endure another day. I mentally checked through the list of each family member and how my death might affect them. I thought of my husband. *Oh, he hates me anyway; he'd probably be relieved.* Two children were already married. I checked them off the list, but when I got to the youngest who were still at home, I knew that they still needed me. I sobbed, wretched with the knowledge that there would be no escape from my misery. Although my existence was useless, my death would bring added misery to innocent people and that wasn't fair to them. I had no choice but to endure.

I made my decision to return home and felt what I can only describe as a darkness, a presence, an entity with me in the car. Perhaps it had been with me all along, but I didn't perceive it until that moment when it raged with fury. I don't know what it was, but I could feel that it hated me with a loathing passion and wanted me dead. It was angry that I had chosen to carry on. The experience frightened me enough to momentarily pull me out of my despair and I was able to drive home.

So I endured. I existed. I perfunctorily performed my responsibilities and tried to hide my pain. This must have been the way my mother felt as she raised me in her broken state. I shuddered to think of the damage I was inflicting on the next generation, but I was honestly doing my best.

I hid from other people like prey hides from predators. I was not safe anywhere.

A person who has never endured this can never fully understand the effort it takes to pretend to be normal. I was filled with anxiety and dreaded any social encounters. The innocent question, "How are you?" was the most excruciating experience. I pretended and lied. I lived in fear of exposure because I was a fraud. I avoided social situations and was constantly looking for an escape route. I hid from other people like prey hides from predators. I was not safe anywhere.

A good day was one in which I didn't wish to cease existing. I had those sometimes; the depression seemed to come in waves. When I was down there was no joy; there was no hope. I could see a beautiful sunset, or smell a fragrant rose, or hear a child's laughter and feel absolutely nothing. Happiness doesn't come from circumstances; it comes from within, and within I was empty. I lived in that place for five years.

In the past I had always been able to find joy in forgetting myself and serving others, but every time I tried to serve, I failed.

When my two year-old grandson found a marker during his supposed naptime, he covered the walls, the sheets on his bed, and everything else he could reach with green artwork. I thought, *Well, here is something I can do. I can at least wash walls.*

I searched on the internet to find the best method of marker removal and armed myself with washcloths, paper towels, Magic Erasers, etc. and headed to my daughter's home. I had texted beforehand to let her know that I was coming, but when she opened the door, she was surprised to see me.

"I'm so sorry. I can't visit today," she said. "I have a doctor's appointment and I'll be leaving soon."

"You didn't know I was coming? I guess you didn't get my text." I replied. "Well, that's okay. I can clean while you're away."

"Clean? What are you going to clean?" She looked puzzled.

"I put it in my text. I came to clean the marker off the walls and wash the marker off the sheets."

"Oh," she seemed slightly embarrassed for me. "I already cleaned the walls and the sheets are in the washer."

"I'm sorry I didn't get here in time."

I gave her a hug and returned to the car, carrying my basket of supplies and trying not to cry.

Another failed opportunity came to help serve in a canning factory which provides food to feed the poor and needy; I gathered my courage and signed up. When I received the text that they had enough help and didn't need me, I cried.

Another opportunity arose and I tried again. I arrived at the canning factory, received the training, and washed and put on the hairnet, apron and gloves. That day they were canning cream of mushroom soup. Volunteers were assigned various stations and I was among two volunteers assigned to the initial step, actually preparing the soup mixture in a large vat which would then be sealed into cans. A trained overseer walked us through each step, working with us as we followed the instructions written on a clipboard. As each step was completed we were to put our initials next to the step indicating that we had completed that part and marking the time.

Something went wrong with a batch of soup and there were lumps. They had to halt the whole production line, throw out that batch of soup, and make a new one. Guess who's signature was on that batch of soup? Mine. The workers were very kind and assured me that it wasn't my fault, but I knew that it really was. I was a Jonah. I was bad luck and should be thrown overboard for the good of humanity.

In the past, whenever I got overwhelmed, my husband Lewis would encourage me to back off and not take on too much. His advice was kindly meant, but the message I always heard was, "Quit. Give up. What you're doing doesn't make any difference anyway." It made me angry.

After so many failed attempts, I knew that he was right all along: my help was neither wanted nor useful. Service, which had once been a lifeline to happiness and fulfillment, was no longer an option. I was useless. I was completely trapped with no method of escape in sight. I had no hope of deliverance.

THE INVITATION

When I first saw the email from my sister Suzanne with an invitation to attend a women's retreat, I recoiled in horror. The idea of being surrounded by people day and night with no means of retreat or escape filled me with anxiety. I wouldn't even open the email; the subject was terrifying enough. I quickly put it out of my mind.

A few days later, when I finally dared open the email, I learned that my sister wasn't just inviting me to this retreat, she was hosting it. She said she felt inspired that it was something she needed to do. I printed the attachment and read:

"Remembering You"
All-inclusive women's retreat at the Marriott Mountainside Resort in Park City.
A Happy Home Begins with YOU!

- Come enjoy a rejuvenating and relaxing 3-day/3-night women's retreat
- Be inspired with 12 hours of enlightening training and engaging activities
- Recharge yourself mentally, emotionally, spiritually and physically
- Gain greater awareness of your amazing identity and power within
- Learn how to experience greater peace and happiness today and always
- Acquire tools and techniques to create the life and relationships you want
- All while enjoying this beautiful resort nestled among nature and mountains

No, thank you. It would not be a "rejuvenating and relaxing" retreat; it would be a nightmare. Although the topics sounded like something I needed, I had no hope that anything would actually make a difference. Besides, there's no way I could endure being that close to people without an escape. It took tremendous effort to make it through a single conversation without falling apart; there was no way I could survive three days. I'd love to support my sister, but I couldn't do that.

A few days later my mother stopped by to talk with me about the women's retreat. I learned that my mother, who had taken up painting in her retirement years, had been recruited to be one of the guest speakers at the retreat. Her topic was "Seeing your place in the big picture: You matter." All the attendees were going to paint a picture together as a part of the therapy.

I had no hope that anything would actually make a difference.

Oh great, now I felt even more guilt. Since I was keenly aware of how it feels not to be supported and to prepare and have no one show up, I made a great effort to support others. Now it would not only be my sister I was letting down, but also my mother. I didn't want to go, but I felt guilty.

My mother gave me a copy of a more detailed agenda for the retreat. I read:

"Woman is that she might have joy!"
You won't want to miss these powerful and uplifting topics:
- Loving yourself - learn why this is "key" to truly loving others
- Improving your relationship with "self and God"
- Learn powerful techniques to better connect with, and receive answers from our Father in Heaven
- Learn how to overcome our natural tendency to compare, and why this is so important, as it

interferes with your relationships and happiness
- Come to know your true identity
- Come to love and appreciate your body
- Understand the need to be your own "cheerleader"
- Learn tools and techniques to increase your energy and happiness
- How to heal and improve your marriage
- How to better connect with your children - they need you!
- The four different "energy types" and how they affect relationships
- Seeing your place in "The Big Picture" - you matter!
- How to achieve your goals and experience the joy of success
- Understanding "Natural Laws" and how they empower you
- Realize the power to create the life you want!

The material sounded like something that I needed, although I doubted that anything would actually help me. Nothing could help me. I was trapped with no possible escape.

"When is the retreat?" I inquired. She answered.

"Oh, I'm not sure I can come," I said, relieved that I might have a legitimate excuse not to go. "My daughter is expecting a baby and that's just a few days after her due date. Her babies come late, so I'll probably be helping her then."

"Well, that's okay. I know you're all right and don't need this, but do you know of anyone else who does?" she inquired.

I cocked my head slightly. "Am I?"

She laughed. I must have been a better actress than I thought if I could convince my own mother that I was all right.

Now if I could just get her to leave before I fell apart and blew my cover.

But she didn't leave yet. She wanted to talk about sleeping arrangements just in case I did go.

"I don't understand," I said. "Doesn't everyone get their own room?"

"No, Suzanne rented two, two-bedroom condos which sleep 8 people each, so if you come do you want to share a bed with me?"

Wait, what? Not just share a room, but share a bed? My mind went to the scene in Moby Dick where Ishmael and Queequeg shared a bed; that didn't turn out so well. I didn't think people did that anymore. This nightmare was even worse than I previously thought. No place to escape from other people day or night.

"Um, remember that I probably won't be able to make it," I stammered, trying to hide my repulsion at the idea.

"Okay, but if you can come, I'd like you to be with me." She finally gathered her things to go.

Whew, crisis averted. I thought.

Then my daughter betrayed me by having her baby two weeks early.

EMOTION CODE

My lovely daughter has many virtuous qualities, but patience is not one them. Being miserable in the late stages of pregnancy found her looking up every possible wives tale on how to induce labor early.

When expecting her first child, she heard that garlic induces labor and found a restaurant that serves a "labor inducing pizza" loaded with roasted garlic. It's not listed on the menu, but if you happen to have learned about it by word of mouth, you can order this magical creation. She planned a triple date with two friends who were also in their final weeks of pregnancy and ordered the largest size pizza they had, chowed down, and hoped. One of the three actually did have her baby that night. She was already having contractions before the meal began, so I'm not convinced that the pizza had anything to do with it, but the legend continues. However, it didn't work for my daughter, who headed to the internet for the next sure fire labor inducing trick. She tried taking long walks, castor oil, stripping the membranes, chiropractic adjustments, eating pineapple, etc. Nothing worked to induce early labor, on time labor, or slightly overdue labor. The child was finally born two weeks late.

Now, in the late stages of pregnancy with her second child, she was back to her research.

"Mom, can you drive me to the acupuncturist today?" she asked. "I don't have a car today, but I found a Groupon online so I can get a discount and they say they can stimulate the points that will induce labor."

"Sure, what time is your appointment?" I answered.

She told me and then added, "You should do it too. It will be fun."

"I'm in," I replied.

I've had acupuncture before to help with vertigo, and it was very effective.

We drove to the acupuncturist, one I had never met before, and began filling out paperwork. When it came to the question, "What is the reason for your visit?" I hesitated. If I wrote 'depression and anxiety,' my daughter might see it and my cover would be blown, and yet, that was the help I needed. I took a deep breath and wrote it on the paper.

He worked on my daughter first, verifying how far she was along to ensure that the baby was fully developed and ready before proceeding.

"Don't be disappointed if nothing happens today," he reassured her. "It usually takes 24-48 hours before labor begins."

He read through my paperwork, and read the part that I hoped to keep secret, aloud.

24-48 hours? Yeah, right. I thought. *It will probably be another 14-28 days.* But I was willing to go along with it since it wasn't going to hurt anything.

Then is was my turn. He read through my paperwork, and read the part that I hoped to keep secret, aloud.

"Depression and anxiety?" I nodded shyly and he went on, "These types of problems usually have an emotional basis and might be better helped another way. I offer other services in addition to acupuncture. Have you ever heard of The Emotion Code and The Body Code?"

"Yes, my sister is actually certified in The Emotion Code and The Body Code," I replied. "I think it sounds awesome, but my husband thinks it's all baloney."

He smiled. "I've had a lot of experience helping people, and I can assure you that it's not baloney. If you ever want to come back and try that, just let me know."

He performed the acupuncture and sent us on our way.

Dr. Butler's words kept echoing in my mind and brought to the surface thoughts that I had previously repressed into oblivion. He reintroduced the idea of The Emotion Code.

The Emotion Code was developed by renowned holistic physician and lecturer Dr. Bradley Nelson. He teaches that emotionally-charged events from your past can still be haunting you in the form of trapped emotions, which are emotional energies that literally inhabit your body. The Emotion Code is a process of identifying and releasing those trapped emotions.

When my sister Suzanne first introduced the idea to me, I was intrigued. She was using The Emotion Code to help her daughter heal from the emotional trauma of being caught in a devastating typhoon in the Philippines and planned to continue her training and open her own practice to help others. I loved the idea of being able to help people heal and wanted to join with her.

I purchased Dr. Nelson's initial package of books and training materials, but my husband wanted me to have nothing to do with it. He thought it was a fraud and researched earnestly on the internet to discredit it.

"That 'hoogie-poogie' makes me sick," he declared.

By the time my materials had arrived in the mail, it was already a taboo topic at our house. In order to preserve a semblance of peace in our home, I sadly forwarded the package to another friend who I hoped would be able to use it, but I deeply resented being stymied and having my beliefs mocked and ridiculed.

I hadn't been able to think about The Emotion Code or The Body Code without shame, regret, jealousy and anger, so I tried not to think about it at all. It became a taboo topic to me, as well. If my sister ever mentioned her practice at family gatherings, I had to leave the room. Having the acupuncturist remind me that it existed and adding testimony to its effectiveness was actually painful. I tried to re-forget it.

We scheduled a second acupuncture session for my daughter for the following Monday, since neither of us thought the first session would actually induce labor, but she hoped to at least start dilating so her doctor would allow her to be induced the following week. However, to our utter amazement, she wasn't able to make the second appointment. She had the baby that weekend. Labor had indeed started about 48 hours after her acupuncture visit. One of her have-the-baby-early schemes actually worked.

AFTERSHOCK

The same day that this beautiful, perfect granddaughter was born, I received yet another aftershock of my personal earthquake. This one was severe enough that it even rattled my unflappable husband. *This is never, ever going to end.* I despaired.

The next day was Monday. I kept my composure as I took my daughter to school, but on the drive home I sobbed inconsolably.

"God please help me!" I cried out. "I can't do this anymore. Please deliver me!"

After a few moments I did feel a little calmer and stopped crying. I remembered the appointment for the acupuncturist and decided to go.

This time I asked for both acupuncture and The Emotion Code. I didn't tell him anything about my circumstances.

The Emotion Code identifies not only the trapped emotions, but the approximate time that the emotion became trapped. Often a childhood event will come up as a cause for a trapped emotion and the event needs to be addressed in some way before it can be released; in this instance, he addressed emotions such as humiliation, depression, anxiety, overwhelmed, worry, crying and a host of other things and they were all from right then.

"That's really unusual," he said. "You must have a lot going on right now."

"Yes, I do." I replied without adding further detail. After the session, I felt a bit lighter and was able to function throughout the day a little better. I was able to think a little clearer and was noticing some improvement, but a single visit didn't solve all my problems.

As we struggled through this latest aftershock, my husband mentioned something about the need of being able to talk through this latest development and not keep these feelings trapped inside.

"I don't have anyone to talk to," I replied.

"You could talk to me," he offered.

"No, thank you. I've made that mistake before," I muttered softly, hoping that he wouldn't hear. He did.

I should have kept my mouth shut, and usually I'm very, very good at keeping my mouth shut, but this time my true feelings slipped out.

I didn't feel safe with him. I didn't feel safe with anyone, but especially not him. I retreated and hid from everyone, and he was the hardest person to hide from since we slept in the same room. I didn't talk because I didn't want to be told that I was wrong, or how I should be feeling, or have my thoughts belittled, or mocked, or dismissed as being unimportant or wrong. I didn't feel supported by anyone, but especially not by him.

> *I should have kept my mouth shut, but this time my true feelings slipped out.*

Perhaps it was my slip of tongue that inspired his "intervention." A few days later I found myself trapped while he forced me to listen to him read an article about depression and demanded that I admit to it and get help. He wanted me to go to a doctor and get diagnosed and begin taking medication.

I felt like a trapped squirrel fighting for my safety. I vacillated between wanting to escape and wanting to lash out at my attacker. He emphasized that couples with a depressed spouse are nine times more likely to divorce, and ended with a threat that he had had enough and that he was done.

"You're done? Fine, go ahead and leave me," I spat. "You could probably do better anyway." I finally escaped the room.

I imagined my life without him and assumed that he would get the kids and the house and I would fade from their lives to live alone in poverty and isolation. It wasn't a pleasant thought, but it seemed easier in some ways than pretending to be okay. I should just give in and embrace the misery; my life would no longer be a lie.

After some space, I began to think about what he said. I was sorry that my depression was affecting anyone else. I had tried so hard to keep it to myself and retreat into invisibility so it wouldn't hurt another soul. I knew perfectly well that I had a problem, but everything I had tried had failed. I couldn't get out on my own; I did need help, but I didn't want the kind of help that he was offering. I had friends who were on antidepressants; they were not the magic bullet that my husband hoped they were.

I knew that sometimes there is a chemical imbalance and medication is the miracle that solves the problem, and that it wonderful; but I also knew that for some, it just adds to the rollercoaster of emotion. They try a new medication and wait for six weeks to see if it's effective; then when it fails, they try another one and continue the process indefinitely with marginal success. I have also done research and some studies say that walking and physical activity are as effective as antidepressants to improve mood and are actually more effective as a long term solution. I think antidepressants are wonderful in some cases, but often overused as a panacea for all situations.

Besides, I knew that the source of my problem was not a chemical imbalance, but a series of life changing events. To me, being diagnosed and taking medication felt like giving up and giving in. How ironic and hypocritical to say that right after wondering if I should give up and give in to embracing my misery. I was a fool.

Taking medication and still being able to live in my house and see my children would be better than refusing it and losing everything. *I guess I'm just being proud and foolish,* I thought. *If that's what I need to do, then I guess I'll do it. I just wish that there was something that could actually heal me rather than chemically masking what I could not hide through willpower alone. Wouldn't it be wonderful not to have to mask anything? Wouldn't it be wonderful not to pretend that I'm not depressed, or to be chemically induced to not be depressed, but to actually be happy? If only that were possible.*

I decided to return to the acupuncturist and had another session of both acupuncture and The Emotion Code. I felt the weight of some of the emotional burden removed and I was lighter. I was ready for another conversation with my husband.

We are not a yelling, fighting couple; there was usually peace in our home. Any time we have an argument of any kind, it affects me deeply. The next conversation following any altercation is especially difficult. Emotionally charged words always exacerbate any situation, and it takes a lot of self control and humility to be able to ameliorate the situation instead. This time I was going to have to set aside my pride and agree to setting up a doctor's appointment and probably begin taking medication. Deep breath. I could do this.

"I didn't mean what it sounded like," he began, "I'm not going to leave you. I'm not going to give up on you. I'll stay with you until the end."

"Thanks," I replied, greatly relieved by the way this conversation was starting. "I know that I have a problem and I'm sorry that it's affecting you. I am trying to do something about it. I'm exercising every day, I've been going to an acupuncturist, I downloaded the 'Headspace' app and have been using that to do guided meditation each day. I am making an effort. I'm really trying."

We embraced, both feeling lighter and more hopeful.

The medication topic hadn't come up in that conversation and I thought that maybe I could try what I was doing a little longer, in hopes that it would make a difference.

You may have noticed that I did not mention that The Emotion Code was part of my current treatment; I did not want him to shoot it down or demand that I go to a different practitioner who didn't offer such nonsense. I knew that it was helping.

I remembered my sister's upcoming women's retreat and stressed over whether or not I dared to go. I was terrified of falling apart and being exposed as a fraud, but I needed to take additional steps to heal and maybe there might be something that would help me, but could I endure it?

RETREAT

Finally, I gathered enough courage to text my sister.

"It looks like I will be able to come."

"Wonderful!" she replied, "Will you be here for the whole retreat and sharing a bed with Mom, as she told me earlier?"

I panicked a bit, but tried something that I would not previously have dared to do. I explained how I felt.

"I don't know. I'm torn. I want to support you and Mom, but I'm not in a good place emotionally and social situations are stressful and painful. Wherever I am I want to escape and I'm afraid of staying there with no place for retreat. Honestly I don't want to go at all, but I know you and Mom have put so much effort into preparing. I don't want to fall apart in front of you, in front of strangers. I don't think I can do this."

Almost as soon as the text was sent, the phone rang. I hesitated, took a deep breath, and answered it. It was, of course, my sister.

"Linda, you don't need to come to support me," she began. "You don't have to come if you don't want to. This isn't about me; it's about the people who want to come and learn how to be happy and get more out of life. I would never force anybody to come."

Relief coursed through my body at being given permission that I didn't need to go. I wasn't being forced or guilted into anything. I had a choice. That was what I needed to hear, although I didn't know it until that moment.

"I'm so sorry that you're going through a difficult time. I would never know it by looking at you. You always seem so calm and put together," she said.

"That's because I'm a fraud," I said, beginning to cry. "People think I have it all together, but I'm really a mess."

"I've felt that way before, too. People thought I had it all together and all the while I was miserable inside. I thought there was no way out and I'd just have to endure for the rest of my life," she added. "But now I'm genuinely happy. It's so freeing. It's wonderful."

Wait, what? Did my sister just say that she thought she would have to 'endure' for the rest of her life? That word struck me since that was exactly how I was feeling, and I couldn't believe that my sister, my perfect sister who is tall and thin and confident and driven and successful, could ever have felt that way. I have both admired her and envied her my entire life. It surprised me, but also comforted me that perhaps she wouldn't judge me, and gave me a sliver of hope that she might even be able to help me.

Perhaps she wouldn't judge me. [It] gave me a sliver of hope that she might even be able to help me.

"We'll be talking about tools that people can use to increase energy and happiness, and how to achieve goals and experience the joy of success," she continued. "It's going to be awesome. Does that sound like something that you might like?"

"Well, yes." I stammered. "Maybe."

"Some people are just coming during the day and going back home at night. Some are coming for all three days, and others are coming for only one or two days. Others are staying at the condo the whole time. There are lots of options. What sounds best to you?"

"I'm not sure," I said.

"Do you need some time to think about it?" she asked.

"Yes." I sighed with the relief of not having to make a decision right away.

"Linda, I'm a mentor now. I help people achieve their goals, so I'm going to ask you to do something. I'm going to ask you to pick a day that you'll be ready to make a decision. How much time do you need? By what day can you make a decision?"

I was taken aback. I had never had anybody ask something like that before. I thought for a few seconds.

"Sunday. I think I could make a decision by Sunday."

"Excellent!" she replied. "What time on Sunday?"

"Uh, maybe by noon?" I offered.

"I'm going to be busy until 3:00. Will you call me with your decision at 3:00 on Sunday?"

"Um, okay. I think I can do that," I said. We both said our goodbyes and hung up, and somehow the idea of going didn't seem so repugnant anymore.

By Sunday at 3:00, I had decided to go. I was still scared, but I now felt like my sister was on my side, and having one person that I didn't need to hide from helped me to feel a bit safer. She offered a plan to allow me an escape if I needed one; I could be on the food committee, which could provide me with an excuse if I felt I needed to leave at any time during the retreat. I gratefully accepted the position.

A few days later it was time to go. Since there was limited parking at the condo, I would be carpooling with my mom. We arrived in time so I could help prepare breakfast for those who had come up the night before. After cleaning up the breakfast dishes, it was time to begin.

THE RETREAT - DAY 1

The next three days were akin to drinking out of a fire hose. There was so much information that although I was taking notes as fast as I could, I knew that I didn't understand most of it enough to be able to apply it. I'll share a few highlights here, and then go into more detail later on as I actually started to put them into action.

Suzanne began by sharing her story of how she met and fell in love with her handsome husband. But, soon after their marriage, a series of events and miscommunications built walls between them. They were committed to staying together but neither felt safe or understood by the other.

Other life events compounded her burden. In one instance a person came to her house and criticized her so severely that after this person left, she crumpled to the ground, too weak to hold herself up. She sobbed inconsolably and thought she'd never recover.

I could empathize with that feeling. I, too, had been crumpled on the ground in sobbing, inescapable misery. I felt sad that Suzanne had endured such a horrible experience, but I also felt something else; I felt like I was not alone. If she had felt that way and recovered, then perhaps there was hope for me.

She talked about her experience being introduced to The Emotion Code/Body Code and how she had helped her daughter overcome the trauma of being caught in a devastating typhoon in the Philippines. She wanted to be able to help her husband overcome the trauma from his tragic upbringing (both his parents had died when he was still young), but he wouldn't have anything to do with it.

"Shocking, isn't it?" she laughed with exaggerated sarcasm. "He didn't want me to 'fix' him. Nobody wants to be controlled or manipulated or 'fixed,' even when we think it's for their good. The only one we have power to change is ourselves."

She talked about being introduced to trainings by Kirk Duncan, owner of "3 Key Elements," where she learned about mentoring and how to help people make lasting changes in their lives through empowerment and release techniques. He opened her eyes to what she had been missing—a way to find and heal the roots of these negative emotions and then replace them with positive high energy. She continued with additional training and wanted to expand her business to help others more effectively, but the thought came to her that she couldn't help others until she had healed herself and her marriage first.

The only one we have power to change is ourselves.

So she dedicated herself to self-healing. She worked with a mentor and spent an hour or more a day applying the tools and techniques that she had been taught.

"It has been nearly a year since I made that decision, and it has changed my life. Where would you like to be a year from now?"

She talked about feeling compelled, almost against her will, to attend a women's retreat, and at the conclusion a single thought overpowered her: "Now it's your turn. You need to host a retreat."

So she began to act, first creating an image in her mind of what she wanted the event to be like. She made an audio recording of her "after story," the story she hoped to see fulfilled in the future.

"I wanted it to be in a beautiful place," she said, "I wanted a picture window view of the mountains with blue sky, sunshine, and a few wispy clouds. I wanted 20 women to attend who needed to be here and that I would have something of value for each of them. In my recording, I'm not wishing for it to be so, I'm speaking as if it already happened. I listened to my recording every day and acted to make it happen. I did my best, but it wasn't enough. A few weeks ago, very few had signed up and I was worried that it would be a flop. I apologized to my husband because I had invested our money into reserving these condos with no apparent hope of recovering costs. My husband is very budget conscious and carefully scrutinizes our purchases. I thought I'd be in trouble, but was surprised by his answer, 'I don't care about the money. You have healed our home. You are able to defuse any conflict in our home and you can even defuse me. I am so grateful for what you've done for our family. What you're doing is such a wonderful thing and I support you 100%.'"

I was in awe. I couldn't even imagine what it would be like to have that kind of support and understanding from my husband.

"Even though things didn't look like they would work, I kept moving forward as if they would," she continued. "Then right before the retreat was to begin, things began to fall into place and here we are. Look around the room. We had 22 people signed up and 2 weren't able to make it, so that makes 20, which is exactly what I asked for. Look out that wall *We're not helpless victims, resigned to simply endure.* of windows at the mountain and notice the blue sky and sunshine and those wispy little white clouds over there. The 'after story' that I had created in my mind is coming to pass. Thank you so much for coming and for helping to create this beautiful experience we're sharing together."

She taught that we're not helpless victims, resigned to simply endure. We have the power to create the life that we want, a life of happiness, and there are three basic keys to happiness: identity, relationships, and progression.

"We each have our own unique energetic balance made up of the positive and negative emotions we are filled with. The positive emotions are like deposits and the negative like withdrawals from a bank account," she said as she drew an outline of a person on a large pad of paper set up on an easel, filling the outline with plus signs and minus signs.

"If we have a lot of positives and a few negatives, we have a high energy balance allowing us to live an energized, happy, and fulfilled life. If we have a low level of positives with a lot of negatives, we are left with a low energy balance that leaves us feeling low self-esteem, depressed, and drained. Now take each of the different aspects of our identity: physical, spiritual, mental, emotional, and social, and write down how you feel your current balance is in each area. Is it high or low? Which areas could use some improvement?"

I looked down at the figure that I had drawn in my own notebook, and knew the answer wasn't good. I had a low balance in every area.

"If you want to improve your balance, then you need to add positives and get rid of negatives. It isn't enough to just get rid of the negatives," she drew a horizontal line with a dip in it.

"There is a law called the Law of the Vacuum. Nature abhors a vacuum and whenever we have a hole or a void, it naturally tends to fill up with negative, because negative thoughts and emotions are so prevalent and all around us."

"I am trained in The Body Code, where I help people identify and release negative emotions, and I've had a lot of success. Yet I was baffled that I needed to clear the same negative emotions from my clients over and over again. It wasn't until I learned about the Law of the Vacuum that I understood that although removing the negative is a necessary element of healing, it isn't enough. You have to add positive thought and emotions."

She shared several ways we could this through nature, exercise, music, and serving others. "During this retreat I'm going to teach you a few more simple tools to increase your positive balance in your emotional bank account. We'll start with 'declarations.'"

She paused to take a sip of water.

"One thing you don't ever want to say is, 'What's wrong with me?' because your subconscious will start searching."

"'Okay,'" she said mimicking a subconscious voice, "'she wants to know what's wrong with her. Search all programs to locate all her faults,' and it will find them. Don't ever say that again. Instead say, 'What did I do right today?' and the subconscious will get to work searching for what you did right. This helps promote that positive emotional balance."

She tore off the sheet of paper that she'd been drawing on and started a new page.

"Okay, I want to explain the Law of Vibration," she said and began to explain that The Law of Vibration states that anything that exists in our universe, whether seen or unseen, broken down and analyzed in it's purest and most basic form, consists of pure energy or light which resonates and exists as a vibratory frequency or pattern. All matter has its own vibrational frequency. The thoughts, feelings and actions we choose

One thing you don't ever want to say is, 'What's wrong with me?' because your subconscious will start searching.

also have their own particular rates of vibration. Our energy can move at a very high vibrational frequency, which will bring us more health, happiness and prosperity, or at a very low vibrational frequency, which will bring us the opposite. Emotions like shame, guilt, apathy, and depression have very low vibrational frequencies while positive emotions like love, joy and peace have very high vibrational frequencies.

"Sometimes you can feel the vibrations of another person, although you may not realize that's what you're feeling," she said.

"Have you ever had someone walk in the room and you could just feel they were angry without their saying a single word? How about when someone enters a room and they're radiating happiness and excitement? What you're feeling is the vibration of that emotion emanating from the person."

Next she talked about the Law of Attraction, the belief that by focusing on positive or negative thoughts a person brings positive or negative experiences into their life. What we send out comes back to us amplified and multiplied.

"If we're sending out thoughts or vibrations of worry, then it comes back multiplied as anxiety," she said. "If we send out thoughts or vibrations of sadness, then it comes back multiplied as depression."

I wasn't sure I liked that answer; it's so much easier to blame outside circumstances.

I paused to think about that. I had been extremely worried and devastatingly sad, which had indeed grown into anxiety and depression. Was I really attracting anxiety and depression? If so then, in a way, I did this to myself. I wasn't sure I liked that answer; it was so much easier to blame outside circumstances. I guessed the flip side of that was that I should be able to have the power to do something about it. *Which do I want more, to be proactive and heal or to be validated in my misery?* That question is so much harder to answer when you're in it than when you're watching from the outside.

Suzanne drew a stick figure on the board surrounded by a circular bubble.

"The space inside this bubble is our 'comfort zone'. The size of our comfort zone can vary greatly from person to person and it can be enlarged or contracted."

She referred to the figure on the board and explained further, "When we struggle with our identity, then our comfort zone collapses. We may not feel comfortable anywhere."

I paused to think about that one, as well. That was certainly true for me. Situations that had once been easy and comfortable were now very painful and uncomfortable. Did that correlate with struggling with my identity?

She circumscribed this bubble with a second, larger bubble.

"This bubble represents our 'growth zone.' We have to step outside of our comfort zone in order to be able to grow. When we step outside our comfort zone into the growth zone, it enlarges our comfort zone. We can choose growth, or we can simply let life do it for us. We're going to grow one way or another. That's what this life experience is all about."

She compared it to a boat without a motor, rudder, or sails being tossed and blown by the wind and the waves. The current and the waves may take us to our destination eventually, but how much better it is when we participate in the steering and propulsion. She took the comparison to another level by suggesting that instead of being tossed as a rudderless boat, we could be flying to our destination in a jet plane.

"Now let's talk about how to increase the energy balance of each different aspect of our identity: physical, spiritual, mental, emotional, and social."

"We're going to begin with our physical identity," she said. "In the journey to love yourself, you need to learn to love your body. Like most women, I have things about my body that I don't love, and although there are many things about it that are wonderful, in the past all I could see were my flaws."

"One day I had an epiphany," she went on. "The thought came to me that my body is not 'me'. My soul or spirit has existed forever, while my body has only existed for a few decades. Compared to my spirit, it's just a baby. I would never treat a baby the way I criticize my body. I learned that I need to love and nurture it like a child. I need to be kind to my body. Those aspects that I didn't love before are still there, but they don't bother me anymore. I can honestly say that I love my body. It is perfect. Not in the way that the magazines would define perfection, but it is perfect for me. Your body is perfect for you. Our bodies are wonderful and beautiful, and we should love and care for them."

Then she listed on the board some of the things we could do to nurture our bodies. The food that we eat is the fuel or energy for our body to use. She emphasized that food that is alive gives more energy, so fresh vegetables and fruits obviously give more energy than cooked and processed food. This is another place where we need to add positive and get rid of negative in order to have a positive balance in our body.

Water is necessary. Energy flows through water. A general rule to determine how much water our body needs is to weigh ourselves and divide that number in half. That determines how many ounces of water our body needs to function optimally. For most people, it's about eight, eight ounce glasses per day.

Getting adequate sleep is necessary for our bodies and is crucial for healing. Exercise is important. Caring about our appearance is important.

"You have to get up, shower, get ready, put on your makeup and fix your hair. It matters," she emphasized. "It affects the way you feel."

"Another thing we can do to nurture our body is by releasing negative energies. This can be done through The Body Code, but you can do it yourself through writing letters to our body and then writing your body's response back. You can write to your body in general or to specific parts. Write until you can't think of anything else to say and then move the pen to the next line and wait. Ideas will come to your mind. Just write them down. This is your body's response. We're going to try that now. Take out a new piece of paper. I'll give you a few minutes to write whatever you feel about your body."

She played soft music while giving us time to write.

BODY SHAME

My letter began, "Dear body, I'm not sure where to begin. I'd like to thank you for sight. I am thankful to be able to see the beauties of nature and to be able to see my family. I am thankful for my eyes."

I continued with gratitude for the senses and everything I could think of, but the time ran out before I finished and I certainly didn't have time to write my body's 'response.'

Later that day, after classes were over, the ladies wanted to socialize in the hot tub. The condo has a beautiful series of hot tubs, all of varying temperatures, connected by waterfalls. I purposefully had not brought a swimming suit because I had no intention of socializing, but when I declined, explaining that I hadn't brought a suit, my mother undermined my plan by saying that she had brought an extra and offered it to me.

I felt the peer pressure to join, but to say that the borrowed suit was unflattering on me is an understatement of epic proportion. I wanted to hide and disappear. It was not a relaxing soak for me at all.

When I felt a reasonable amount of time had passed not to cause offense, I quickly wrapped up in a towel and headed back to my room. After I dried, I grabbed my notebook with my unfinished letter to my body and scribbled, "I got in the hot tub today with the ladies and I was so ashamed of you. Why do you need to be so fat?"

I had tried to be positive in my letter, but I guess my true feelings about my body are very negative. I had a long way to go to "love my body." Was that really possible?

After talking about the physical aspects of identity, Suzanne moved to the spiritual aspects of identity. She talked about the principles of agency and accountability. Agency is choice, and it is the power to create the life we want. She drew a series of concentric circles on the board. In the center circle she wrote, "Self and God."

"When we're establishing our identity, we have a tendency to compare ourselves with others, but in order to have a solid foundation for self worth, it really needs to start with our relationship with God. We can't look sideways for our identity. We need to look up," she explained. "We need this basis in order to love ourselves in a healthy way, not prideful, but with a sincere contentment that we are children

I didn't want to write anything. Me and God weren't on good terms.

of God and that He loves us. With that foundation of self worth, we are free to love ourselves without reservation. Once we love ourselves, then we are free to love others as children of God," she said, pointing to that center circle.

Then she wrote on the next layers of circles: family, friends, neighbors, mankind.

"We need to make sure our lives are centered on the inner circle, like clay on a potter's wheel, and then we are able to keep the other relationships healthy and balanced. We need to first love ourselves, then we are better able to spread that love to our family, friends, neighbors, and all mankind."

She asked us to write three questions in our notebooks and gave us a few minutes to answer them.

1) What are my thoughts about myself and my relationship to God?

2) What are my thoughts about God?

3) What are my thoughts about what God thinks of me?

I didn't want to write anything. Me and God weren't on good terms. My answers mostly included that I felt insignificant to him and that He felt indifferent towards me.

Then she said that our relationship with God was based on our thinking.

Shocker. I thought angrily. *That's my fault, too. Just put it on my tab.*

Then she gave suggestions and tools to improve our spiritual identity and our relationship with God. As with every aspect of identity, we needed to remove the negative and add positive. In order to remove the negative she suggested that we have a "complete conversation" or "energetic conversation" with God (or a "higher power" if you're more comfortable with that).

I didn't quite understand what a "complete conversation" or "energetic conversation" meant. It was something about having a conversation with God and telling Him how you felt, dumping everything, and then saying sorry and apologizing for feeling that way and asking for forgiveness. She assured us that doing this wouldn't offend God, since it's done with the intent to heal. The "complete conversation" also helps in adding positive since it includes asking for forgiveness.

Other things to add positive include writing a gratitude journal. She challenged us to write one hundred things that we're grateful for.

I had mixed feelings as I listened since I had tried some of those things in the past with mixed results.

She also recommended meditation and prayer and gave us a tool to get more out of our scripture reading. She called it "scripture instant messaging." Scripture instant messaging includes writing down a question and saying a prayer before beginning to read, then looking for answers to that question as you read the scriptures. The answer may be in the words on the page, or themes, or simply thoughts that come to your mind as you read.

I had mixed feelings as I listened since I had tried some of those things in the past with mixed results. In particular, I had tried writing a gratitude journal, writing a list of five things I was grateful for each night before going to bed. It started out okay, but it was in the midst of this experiment that my first personal earthquake hit.

I can look in my gratitude journal and see the exact date of my last entry, May 31, 2012. The following day as my world shattered, I couldn't think of anything to be grateful for. I never wrote in it again. Now, unfortunately, I associated my gratitude journal with my world falling apart. I was trying so hard to be good and do good, and this is what happened? The thought of that experience just fueled my anger towards God. This whole "spiritual identity" thing, trying to re-establish a relationship with God, was going to be a tough one for me.

ENDURANCE PLAN

I was relieved when she finally moved on to the next aspect of identity. To begin her explanation of the mental aspect of identity, Suzanne returned to her personal story.

"My plan was to endure in misery for the rest of my life. I figured that was my lot in life and that I was strong enough to do it. I have since written a 'New Story' of my future life, one that includes peace and happiness with wonderful relationships with my husband, children, and the people around me. It's a good story and I'm loving life, but I can promise you that if I hadn't changed how I perceived my life to be, I would have continued to live out my original story for the rest of my life. We create our own life's experiences. If you don't like the story you're in, then you'd be wise to write a new one."

She drew a circle on the board and wrote the word "thoughts" in it. Then she drew a heart and wrote "feelings" in it. She drew two more circles with the words "actions" and "results."

"Our thoughts, create our feelings," she explained and drew an arrow from thoughts to feelings.

"Our feelings are the fuel that lead to our actions."

She drew another arrow from feelings to actions.

"And our actions lead to our results."

She drew another arrow from actions to results.

"Then this cycle repeats itself, with the results leading to our thoughts again."

She drew another arrow, completing the cycle.

"There are two places in this cycle where we have the greatest power to make changes," she continued. "It's very difficult to change the way we feel, and results just happen, but we can choose to control our thoughts and our actions. These are the two points where we have power. If we don't manage our thoughts it's like getting in a boat and just drifting; in order to steer, you have to control your thoughts. Thoughts are the beginning of change. They are the beginning of obtaining new results. Emotions are our fuel. They are what lead us to our actions. Good fuel leads to good actions."

She drew another picture to illustrate the next analogy. "Our minds are like the soil in a field. If I plant tomatoes in this field, I'm going to reap tomatoes, but if I plant hemlock, I'm going to reap hemlock. If I plant positive thoughts, I'm going to get positive results. On the other hand, if I plant poisonous negative thoughts, I'm going to get negative results. This is called the Law of the Harvest. You will reap what you plant. That's a natural law and goes along with another law that we already talked about, the Law of Attraction, which is that whatever we send out comes back to us amplified and multiplied, just like planting seeds. The result is bigger than the seed we planted."

This is called the Law of the Harvest. You will reap what you plant.

Damn, I thought. *That seems logical and reasonable. That means that I need to make changes. I need to plant new seeds. I've got to quit planting negative thoughts. How do I do that?*

"I want you to write down your top five negative thoughts. These are thoughts that keep coming back at you again and again," she said. "Then I want you to write two new positive responses to counter those negative thoughts."

She gave us a few minutes to think and write, then brought out a plastic bat and a pillow.

"Okay," she said. "I need a volunteer who's willing to share their negative thoughts and positive declarations they'll use to replace them."

A volunteer came forward and handed Suzanne her list.

"Okay," she said. "I'm going to read off one of your old

negative thoughts and toss this pillow at you. You're going to swing the bat and knock that pillow away while you give your new positive answer. Are you ready?"

"You're not good enough!" Suzanne read off the list while tossing the pillow.

"I'm doing the best I can!" the volunteer yelled and swung the bat, knocking the pillow across the room.

"Your house is never clean!" Suzanne yelled as she tossed the pillow again.

"I'm doing more important things!" the volunteer yelled as she swung the bat again.

"You're not perfect. You'll never be perfect!" Suzanne called out as she tossed the pillow a third time.

"I'm good enough!" the volunteer yelled and swung.

"Okay, we'll set down the bat and the pillow," Suzanne said as she gathered up her props. "But this is what I want you to do metaphorically every time one of those negative thoughts comes into your mind. You swat it away with something positive. Have your answers ready and use them over and over again every time those negative thoughts creep back in."

"Now, in our minds we have different levels of thought," she drew a circle on the board and drew a horizontal line dividing it in half. "We have our conscious thought," she wrote conscious on the top half of the circle, "and our subconscious thought."

She wrote 'subconscious' on the bottom half of the circle.

"Our conscious thought is our reasoning. We have agency or control over these thoughts. The subconscious is more like a computer. It is automated and runs on programs that we either inherited or created earlier in our life. For every thought that your conscious mind comes up with, your subconscious runs through a million. It's always busy in the background, taking care of business. The job of your subconscious is to keep you safe, comfortable, and alive. It builds its database of programs on its interpretation of your past experiences. What our subconscious believes is safe constitutes our comfort zone."

"However, the subconscious can have faulty programs," she continued. "They run automatically, even though they're wrong. Ideas like, 'I can't try new things,' 'I always fail,' 'I'm not good enough,' 'I deserve to be poor or mistreated,' come from faulty subconscious programs we either inherited or created earlier in life."

"The good news is that your conscious mind can create new programs, and if you use these new programs consistently, then your subconscious mind can adopt them to override the old ones. The new subconscious programs are just as easy to run as the old faulty ones."

She paused for another sip of water.

"It begins with a plan. Creation is an idea before it becomes a reality. The first step is to decide what you want. Visualize what you want your life to be like. What is your idea of an ideal marriage? What is your idea of an ideal life?"

She gave us a few moments to write down some of the things that we wanted.

LOST VOICE

I wrote.

"I want peace, acceptance, love, identity, safety, connection, happiness, contentment, abundance, and beauty. I want to be useful. I want to be valued."

I might have written more, but it was time for our first guest speaker to begin. Young, beautiful, and vivacious, Erika began discussing the 'emotion' component of our identity by covering the topic, "Finding your voice."

She began with the story of the Little Mermaid, and how the Little Mermaid gave up her voice and needed to get it back.

"We can lose our voice and become disconnected when we stop talking," she said. "I had two traumatic events in my life that caused me to lose my voice. When I was thirteen I was involved in a tragedy, and found myself surrounded by people who accused me and condemned me and crushed me. I learned that if I spoke, those words were used against me, so I must keep my mouth shut. Later I had an emotionally manipulative boyfriend who controlled me and wouldn't allow me to have my own thoughts and feelings. He told me what I was allowed to think and what I was allowed to feel. I learned that I need to keep everything inside in order to be safe, so I swallowed my words, my thoughts, and my feelings."

Until I heard her speak, the thought never occurred to me that I had lost my voice. I didn't speak. In any social situation, with whatever company, wherever I was, I stayed silent. *Why don't I talk?* I wondered. *When did I lose my voice?*

Perhaps it was because I didn't want to engage in conversation where people might ask me questions. Perhaps it was because I felt I had so much to hide. Perhaps it was because I figured I didn't have anything of value to say. Perhaps it was because I assumed people didn't want to listen to me. Perhaps I feared that people would not respect what I had to say, but would ridicule me for it. I kept silent for so long that I didn't even realize that I was doing it. This new thought struck me like an epiphany. I didn't know that I had lost my voice, but now that I realized it was missing, I wanted my voice back. I wanted to be heard. I wanted to matter.

Erika shared two tools that she used to let go of negative emotion and three empowerment tools that she used to build herself up. Again the pattern was to release negative and add positive to create that positive account balance.

I don't understand what these terms mean. It's like they're speaking a foreign language.

"I use complete conversations and what Kirk Duncan calls 'slaying the dragon' to let go of negative emotions," Erika said.

I don't understand what these terms mean, I thought. *It's like they're speaking a foreign language. I hear sounds, but they mean nothing to me. How do I apply these if I don't even understand what it means, let alone how to do it?*

I despaired.

"Slaying the dragon is writing out your feelings on paper and then destroying the paper either by tearing it up or by burning it," she explained. "I personally like the satisfaction I get when I burn them." She laughed.

"You begin by writing this on the top of the page: I feel (blank) about (blank) because… For example, if you're writing about losing your voice, you might write, 'I feel unsafe about communicating because…Then write everything that comes to your mind. Write until you can't think of anything else to write and then move the pen to the next line and wait. Ideas will come to your mind. Just write them down. When nothing else comes to your mind, you know you're done for now. It's time to tear it up or burn it. Whenever you do a written dump, you want to get those feelings out, but you don't want to save them; you want to let them go. The idea is not to fuel the anger or bitterness, but to let it go. Healing comes from acknowledging and letting go."

"I also use 'complete conversations' also called 'energetic conversations' to let go. While 'slaying the dragon' is a way to release through writing, 'complete conversations' are a verbal release. It's like speaking to an imaginary friend. You don't actually have a conversation with the person, but you address their higher self. You imagine asking for their permission to talk to them and then you let them have it. Tell them all the things you've been holding back. You might even be yelling and swearing, and that's a good thing. Just get it all out. When you can't think of anything else to say, then you need to apologize to them for feeling all those negative thoughts and emotions towards them. Apologizing brings healing. I have had multiple complete conversations with that manipulative boyfriend and I told him all the things that I could never tell him when we were together. You can also have complete conversations with yourself. I had a complete conversation with my 13 year-old self. I yelled at her and told her that she ruined my life."

You might even be yelling and swearing, and that's a good thing.

"The 'let go' techniques are used to release negative energy, but additional tools are needed to add positive energy. I call them 'empowerment techniques,'" Erika continued. "I use imagination, singing, and declarations. Imagination and visualization are very powerful. I might look for a picture online of a person talking while smiling and print it out. Seeing that picture helps me be able to imagine myself being able to be happy about talking. Singing is another tool to help empower, and is especially helpful when you've lost your voice."

"'Declarations' are what they sound like. You are declaring something to be true," she explained. "My declarations are 'my words have value' and 'I have the courage to speak my truth.' I repeat these each morning and each night before I go to bed."

"One last thought," she concluded. "Don't be discouraged when you're not able to regain your voice overnight. It took years to get broken; it's going to take time to heal."

Erika's words resonated with me. She said she had lost her voice, but here she was speaking to a group of people. Whatever she was doing to heal was obviously working.

I liked the idea of having tools to heal. Usually you just get the cheerleader talk of 'you can do it.' You're just expected to change the way you think, but no one teaches you how to do it. She used specific tools to let go and other tools to empower. That gives a plan of action, something a person can actually do in order to change. I wasn't sure I understood how to use those tools yet, but I was starting to believe that those tools existed and they may actually help. That meant that I could actually do something about me.

I wasn't sure I understood how to use those tools yet, but I was starting to believe ... they might actually help.

I was also intrigued by her mention of a complete conversation with her 13 year-old self. Events happened at certain ages in my life, and it made sense to be able to deal with those events individually if needed. I was a different person at age six, or twenty, or whenever those events occurred. Furthermore, if I could have a complete conversation with myself at any age then that meant I could also have a complete conversation with someone else at any age. That gave me the possibility of confronting people who had hurt me in the past, but had changed. I'm not angry with who and what they are now, but I still carried anger at how they hurt me before. Somehow this idea freed me to disconnect the person as they are today from the past event.

After Erika sat down, Suzanne rose for the concluding session for the day.

"I want to explain more about declarations and complete conversations," she began.

"Declarations are positive statements about yourself, who you are and what you want to become. Some of the most basic declarations are 'I love myself', 'I know who I am', and 'I am loved.' At first, you may not believe your own declarations.

It may go like this: 'I love myself!', and your subconscious shouts out 'Liar!'

Don't listen to your subconscious; it's running on faulty programs.

'I know who I am!', and your subconscious shouts out 'Yeah, right.'

'I am loved!' and your subconscious shouts out 'That's never going to happen!'

"Don't listen to your subconscious; it's running on faulty programs. It will take a while before it believes those words, but if you keep at it, eventually your subconscious will stop fighting and eventually embrace those declarations."

"I want you to write down five declarations for yourself, print them out, and put them in a place where you can see them. Repeat them three times each morning when you get up and each night before you go to bed. It will only take about two minutes to do," she reassured us.

"The last thoughts that you have before you go to bed are very important since they may go through your mind over and over while you're asleep. Repeating your declarations before you go to bed will help your subconscious make those new pathways and new programs quicker."

"Your nightly routine is very important," she taught. "If you go to bed thinking of all the things that you didn't get done that day, those things will run over and over in your mind while you're sleeping and increase your stress. Instead, start the habit of validating what you did that was good during the day and claiming your successes. You could write a gratitude journal or write down two things that you accomplished that day."

"I want to explain more about complete conversations," she said.

"Why are they called 'complete conversations?'" someone asked. "What does that mean?"

"Good question. We all use a personal filter when we speak to people. We might share some of what we're thinking or feeling, but we hold a lot back. If we told everybody all the things we really feel about them, we wouldn't have any friends left, right?"

We laughed guiltily.

"A complete conversation is your chance to say the rest of what you're feeling. You don't hold anything back. You put it all on the table. Now it's very important to clarify that the person that you're having this conversation with is NOT in the room with you. You are by yourself. You address their higher self as you imagine them in your mind and talk to that. A person's higher self can handle you yelling at them and telling them how you feel, but if you did that to the actual person nothing good would come of it," she warned.

> *You don't hold anything back. You put it all on the table.*

"Complete conversations have a few key components. First you address the person's higher self; second, you dump and let them have it; and third, you say you're sorry and ask for forgiveness. Some people have tried this and say it didn't work. It didn't create any closure or healing, but that's always because they left out that last crucial step of saying sorry and asking for forgiveness. 'But it's not my fault, I didn't do anything wrong, it was all them,' they will say."

She shook her head.

"It doesn't matter; it will not work if you leave out that part. If you can only say, 'I'm sorry, please forgive me for feeling that way,' it will be enough, but you must apologize or it will not bring any healing or closure."

"After you have that three part conversation with the person's higher self, you're not done yet. You need to have another three part complete conversation with God and a another three part complete conversation with yourself. You hear people talk about the need to forgive yourself, and this is a literal way to apply that. It is an important step."

"Now for me personally," Suzanne added. "I have to break down this process even further. In the portion where you have a complete conversation with God, I need to break that down into conversations with each member of the Godhead, because I have a different relationship with God the Father, than with Jesus Christ or the Holy Ghost."

That made sense to me. I hadn't realized it until she said it, but I had a kind of "good cop, bad cop" idea about the Godhead. I was grateful for the Savior's atoning grace, but always felt like God the Father was the one who shoved me under the bus in the first place. When I tried this 'complete conversation' thing, I would break my conversation with God into three parts, as well.

"What do you say in your complete conversation with God?" someone asked. "I wouldn't know what to say."

"Well, remember the three parts of a complete conversation. First, you address God the Father. You don't need to say 'your higher self' because that's His only self. Dump and say whatever you feel, then conclude with something like, 'I'm sorry for feeling that way, please forgive me.'"

"The complete conversation with the Savior might conclude with something like, 'I'm sorry I didn't give this to you sooner. Please forgive me.'"

"Finally the complete conversation with the Holy Ghost might conclude with something like, 'I am sorry for keeping you from me, please forgive me,'" she suggested. "Some of my clients don't believe in God the way that I do, and that's okay. You can simply address a 'higher power' in a similar way. I know that faith isn't fashionable right now, but if you want healing, that spiritual aspect is crucial. There is no other way. Every addiction recovery program includes acknowledging a high power. It is a necessary component of healing."

Interesting, I thought. *These are things I've never thought of doing before.*

"I have one more object lesson before we finish for the day."

She brought out an empty water pitcher on a tray.

"These ping pong balls represent the negative, yucky stuff that you have trapped inside you."

She added several ping pong balls to the pitcher.

"They may be hidden at the bottom, and may not even be bothering you much, but they're in there."

She then added water to the ping pong ball pitcher from a water bottle.

"Adding water represents our efforts to change and fill ourselves with positive. As you begin to add positive you'll notice that those negative things that had settled to the bottom begin to rise to the top. You will remember things that you have buried or maybe even forgotten and you will have to deal with them."

As she filled the pitcher with water, the ping pong balls did indeed rise to the surface.

"However, if you continue to fill yourself with positive, then eventually you will be able to clear the negative."

She continued to fill the pitcher with water until the balls floated up and spilled over the sides of the pitcher leaving it filled with nothing but clean, clear water.

"You need to understand before you begin the process of healing that it will bring up pain and it will be hard. That doesn't mean that you're on the wrong path," she assured us. "When the yuck comes up, just let it go. It is a necessary part of the process of cleaning it out."

"Here's one last thought for the day. We each have our own personal mess and that is the gift that we have to help others. Your mess is your message," she concluded.

Your mess is your message? I mentally repeated. *Well, I'm certainly a mess, perhaps I have a message, too.*

THE RETREAT - DAY 2

"Good morning!" Suzanne called merrily to the assembling ladies. "Let's get some positive energy in the room with some upbeat music."

She found a song on her phone and turned it on.

"I have learned that music is a powerful tool to bring positive energy into our lives and I've been trying to use it more. I've also learned that dancing and moving around is an awesome tool to give us a boost of positive energy! I used to not be able to raise my arms above the level of my head because that was way out of my comfort zone and I just couldn't do it."

She raised her hand with a bent elbow in a timid gesture to demonstrate.

"Now I can reach out and stretch all the way."

She reached her outstretched arms toward the ceiling.

"I never used to dance, but I've learned it's an easy tool I can use any time and in any situation to create the energy I'm seeking. Different types of music are better suited to different types of activities. If I need some energy to be motivated to clean my house, I need bouncy upbeat music playing. If I need to study, think, or be calm, then gentle music is more appropriate. Music is a powerful tool and I'm learning to love it and to incorporate it in my life."

I used to love to dance. I frequently played music and danced around while doing the kitchen chores; it enlivens the mundane into something much more enjoyable. I even had a playlist labeled "Saturday chores" with fun bouncy songs to help us get moving. My grown kids tell me that they still associate certain songs with doing their chores. I hadn't felt much like dancing lately. I missed dancing. I missed wanting to dance.

"Okay, everybody get up and dance with me for one song

and then we'll begin," Suzanne said.

Whoa, that is not what I meant, I thought. I don't want to dance here in front of all these strangers.

Suzanne picked a new song and everybody rose from their seats. As the music began, we moved around awkwardly to the beat. I thought about Suzanne's comment about not being able to raise her arms above her head, and I wondered if I could do it.

A single song can seem very, very long when you're waiting for it to end.

I tried raising my arms high above me. Although I was physically capable of doing that, it was way too awkward and I quickly put them down again.

With elbows bent at my side and my feet moving in a rhythmic side-together-side-together motion, I thought of the movie *Hitch* and Will Smith instructing, "This is where you live. Right here. Elbows six inches from the waist, ninety degree angle…"

A single song can seem very, very long when you're waiting for it to end, but I have to admit that the upbeat song and moving around did help to increase the positive energy in the room.

"Morning is an important time to increase the positive energy so that we can use it throughout the day," Suzanne began. "Some natural energy boosters are music, exercise, nature, and a spiritual boost through prayer, meditation, or reading scriptures. A positive morning routine can give you energy and set the tone for the day."

"Today we're going to begin by discussing the topic of relationships," she said.

She drew an image on the board. It was a repeat of an image that she had drawn the day before, a cycle of words in circles that read: thoughts, feelings, actions, results.

"Our thoughts determine our feelings. Our feelings lead to our actions. Our actions lead to our results," she reviewed. "Remember that the points on the cycle where we have control are our thoughts and our actions. These are the points of power. If we want to change our results, or experience with life. We must change either our thoughts or our actions, and changing both is even better! This is true in every aspect of our lives, and particularly in our relationships."

"When you're interacting with a person, it's important to be present. That means that we stop being busy for a little while and focus on the person," she said. "This has been a difficult change for me. I always want to be busy and look like I'm accomplishing something. I felt that I could listen to somebody and do the dishes at the same time, and maybe make a mental grocery list, and think about all the things I need to accomplish that day. I was there while they were talking. I listened. I did a good job right? I may have been there physically, but the person talking to me probably didn't feel like I was listening or that they were more important than all the other things I had on my mind. I'm learning that busy-ness is not a 'badge of honor.'"

When you're interacting with a person, it's important to be present.

"Also eye contact is very important while listening," she continued. "This shows the other person that you are present and interested in what they have to say."

"Okay, next we're going to talk about the four energy types: air, water, fire, and earth. I used to think that everybody thought about things the same way that I do. I figured all people valued the same things that I value. When I understood the different energy types it opened my eyes and I could see why my husband and children did the things that they did. I had a better understanding of their motivation and their point of view," Suzanne said.

"Each energy type naturally comes with many amazing gifts and strengths. These gifts enrich our own lives, and when combined with those we 'bump' into, we compliment and complete each other to make things even better. As everything has its opposite, each energy type also comes with natural weaknesses. These are the areas we know to be aware of and work to improve within ourselves," she said.

"People with the air energy type are motivated by fun. These people are the life of the party. They are creative and full of new ideas. However, they're not usually good at sticking to tasks. They often lose interest at completing those ideas, because they're already on to the next new idea."

"People with the water energy type are motivated by connection. They love comfort, they can see possibilities and are often very good at detail work. However, they may have a hard time making decisions and tend to worry," she said. "Sometimes they may suffer from 'paralysis by analysis.'"

"People with the fire energy type are motivated by results. These are the people who you can count on to 'get 'er done.' They love to accomplish things and make great leaders. However, they may be concentrating on the task and not be considerate of the other people involved. Also sometimes they don't plan very well, they just act. They tend to go 'ready, fire, aim', rather than 'ready, aim, fire,'" she continued.

"People with the earth energy type are motivated by perfection. They are usually very good at seeing the whole picture. They can take any idea and see how to make it better, how to perfect it. They are analytical and like facts, numbers, and strategies. They see things as being very clearly right or wrong. However, these people tend to be stubborn, as they are their own authority. Because they always think they're right, why would they budge? They can also be critical and judgemental in their desire to perfect people and things. They are particularly hard on themselves," she said, "This energy type describes me. My energy type is earth."

Oh, so that's where that comes from, I thought. Years ago my children introduced me to a fabulous animated series called *Avatar: The Last Airbender* by Nickelodeon. In the series, there are four nations: air, water, fire, and earth. The inhabitants of each nation have a special connection with their element, and some inhabitants have power over their associated element called 'bending.' The inhabitants of each nation also tend to show some of the characteristics that Suzanne was describing, and are typified by the main characters. For example, Toph from the earth kingdom is very stubborn. Zuko from the fire nation is passionate, short tempered and driven by his cause. Aang, the air nomad, is primarily motivated by fun. Katara from the water tribe is often concerned about how people feel and her brother Sokka takes care of the planning and details.

As I've watched the shows and seen the interaction between the characters, I've often thought, *Wow, I'm like Katara and my husband is like Aang.*

In one episode, Sokka says, "Look, I hate to be the wet blanket, but since Katara's busy…" obviously implying that being the "wet blanket" is usually Katara's job. While this interaction is very funny, it also shows another aspect of the water energy type; I was the one with a strong sense of duty who was ready to get back to work, while my husband wanted to flit around and play. Guess which one of us was more fun at home? To be honest, I was jealous of my husband. He was so fun and quirky and creative and the life of the party, and I was a "wet blanket." Next to him, I would always be second rate and invisible.

I was the one with a strong sense of duty who was ready to get back to work.

Having a better understanding of energy types also helped me understand why I struggled feeling "safe" with my husband in all sorts of ways. When it came to finances he doesn't value "stuff";

he valued fun and experience. "The only thing you can take with you is experience," was pretty much his motto. I, on the other hand, wanted security, I wanted a plan. I wanted savings.

When it came to personal safety, I didn't feel secure there either. My husband was very spontaneous. He didn't like to plan. You just went and did it, and if things went wrong and you got stranded or something, that just added to the adventure and the fun. Sometimes I wondered if I accidentally married Hagrid from *Harry Potter*. He was kind and well-meaning, but he had a different idea of safety than most people.

He was kind and well-meaning, but he had a different idea of safety than most people.

For example, when we took a trip to Panama and the nearby San Blas Islands, Lewis was so excited to take me to see the places where he'd lived for two years as a young man. The glitz of the modern high rise buildings in Panama City didn't interest him in the least. It wasn't until we made it to the slums with decrepit cinderblock houses and stray mongrel dogs that he got excited.

"I hope I get to show you the cockroaches and the giant cockroach-eating spiders! They're so fast you won't believe it!" he called out gleefully. We stayed in a pup tent in sleeping bags on a tiny island with no electricity and no water. It truly qualified as "an adventure."

I have to admit that it was a great trip, in part because we did not see the cockroaches and giant cockroach eating spiders.

Okay, so with this new information, I could see where he was coming from. He just wanted to have fun. That's his nature. Those are the gifts and the challenges of his energy type, but this new knowledge didn't magically change me. I still felt jealous and annoyed and unsafe. Why do we tend to marry our opposite?

"It's easy to look at another person and be jealous of their gifts," Suzanne said. "Sometimes we might not recognize our own gifts and the contributions that we make. It takes all four energy types to create a balance. We need the creation, the details, the completion and the perfection to make anything happen. Also remember that just because something doesn't come naturally doesn't mean you can't have that gift. We can always 'aspire to what we admire,' rather than being jealous of another's gifts."

"If you're interested in learning more about energy types there are several books available. I really enjoy the books written by Carol Tuttle. She wrote one called *It's Just My Nature* and another fun book called *Dressing Your Truth* that shows how to dress for your energy type. If we wear the colors, patterns, and style that match our energy type it sends a consistent message, but if we don't, then we send a conflicting message and people naturally respond to that without even realizing it," Suzanne said.

> *Just because something doesn't come naturally doesn't mean you can't have that gift.*

"The first time I dressed my truth and wore a red dress in public, I was terrified that it was too bold and I would look out of place. Instead I received compliment after compliment and no one mentioned the dress at all; they just said that I looked great. I had been dressing in soft colors and shades to try to balance my bold nature, but it didn't work like I thought it would. It had the opposite effect than I'd hoped. Now that I dress my truth, the way I look is consistent with my energy and people tend to accept me as I am. I had to give away nearly all the clothes in my closet and start over, but now I love getting dressed in the morning and I love the way that people treat me," she beamed.

I can add my unsolicited testimonial, that she did look great. She was bright, tailored and professional.

Those clothes would look horrible on me, I thought. *I would disappear and all you'd see is the clothes. I wonder if there's a style that would make me look good, too. I guess I'd better read the book.*

It might be worth a try.

"Okay, so understanding our energy type and the energy types of the people around us are some of the tools that we can use to help us understand another person's point of view," Suzanne explained, "and that leads us to our next topic which is, 'what to do when there are problems in relationships.'"

"Communication is far more challenging than merely speaking our mind," she said. "I might say something that makes perfect sense to me, but another person might understand it completely different than what I intended."

My mind wandered briefly to Shakespeare's plays, which are full of examples of people misunderstanding each other. In some cases, the misunderstanding creates a comical situation and in others, such as *Othello,* the misunderstandings in communication create tragic situations.

What do you think motivated his or her words or actions?

"In order to avoid our own tragic situations we might want to step back and evaluate three things," Suzanne said. "First is point of view. Try to see it from the other person's point of view. Consider what we talked about with energy types. What do you think motivated his or her words or actions? Take time to talk to each other and ask for clarification in how they're seeing it. As you do this it brings greater understanding, which open the door to find resolution."

"Second is miscommunication," she continued. "Remember that he or she might not be interpreting your words the way you meant them, or vice versa. Take the time to clarify your words. Not to drive your point home, but always with the intent to create understanding. The third part is analyzing how the first two things created the problem in the first place. Knowing this can help you eliminate future conflicts."

My mind jumped back to *Othello.* If the characters had

followed these steps, then Desdemona and Othello would have lived happily ever after rather than both ending up dead. This could be useful stuff.

"As healthy, loving relationships are so crucial to our happiness and well being, it would be very wise for each of us to do all we can to heal them," Suzanne said. "Service is another very effective tool to not only heal relationships, but to strengthen our self-worth and create greater connections with others. Serve those you love, and serve other people. When we serve others we forget ourselves, and often the things that were bothering us before somehow don't seem as important anymore. Service is healing."

I felt a twinge of pain at her discourse on service. I used to love to serve because I knew it helped me forget myself and brought me joy, but I had come to believe that my service didn't make a difference and my efforts were unwanted and unappreciated and in some cases actually detrimental. I would like to be able to serve again.

"Another critical tool to healing relationships is forgiveness," Suzanne said.

That can be a tough one, I thought. Like most people, I wanted justice. I'd like the other guy to come to me and say 'I'm sorry' and show me evidence that they were trying to do better before I wanted to forgive them. Just giving 'blanket forgiveness' seemed like they were getting off easy.

Suzanne continued, "Forgiveness is inescapably intertwined with repentance, which means basically showing sorrow and regret for having done wrong. Many people don't want to do this because they figure it is all the other guy's fault. That's rarely the case, but even if it is, we can at least apologize and ask for forgiveness for our feelings towards them."

Wow, I thought. *Now I'm not only supposed to apologize even if I don't think it's my fault, now I'm supposed to ask for forgiveness as well? My unfair-o-meter is going off. This is a tough pill to swallow. Why would I want to do this?*

Suzanne went on.

"That may seem counterintuitive and totally unfair to say we need to forgive someone and apologize when they're the one who hurt us, but it isn't about them; it's about healing yourself."

"Let me explain it this way," she said. "When a person hurts me, it is like he or she threw a harpoon into my heart," she said drawing a stick figure illustration.

"As you know, a harpoon is like a barbed spear that is attached to a long rope. The barb in the harpoon makes it stay inside me and the rope creates an attachment to the other person.

I am not 'letting them off the hook'; instead I am 'letting me off the hook.'

That harpoon will stay inside me until I take it out, and as long as that harpoon is inside me, it is also keeping me connected to the person who hurt me. If I remove the hook through forgiveness, it not only removes the harpoon from me, it also severs my connection to the other person. I am not 'letting them off the hook'; instead I am 'letting me off the hook.'"

That's an interesting perspective, I thought. I'm going to have to chew on that for a while before I'm ready to accept it, though.

"An excellent way to do this is through those 'complete conversations' that we talked about yesterday," Suzanne said. "It's very important to remember that the person that you're having this conversation with is NOT actually anywhere near you. You are by yourself. You might want to go outside or have a conversation while you're driving by yourself. A complete conversation has three separate parts, first you invite the person's higher self to talk to you. The next step is to let them have it. You can yell and cry if you need to, but get it all out, and don't hold anything back. The objective is to get all that garbage out of you, otherwise you're still carrying it around and letting it affect your life. The final step is to apologize and say 'Will you please forgive me?' That last step is very important. If you leave that part out, the complete conversation won't bring the healing you're after."

Oh, I thought. *So I get to apologize to the imagined 'higher self' of the other person? I might be talking to a tree outside, or the steering wheel as I'm driving, or something like that? That won't be as bad as I was imagining before. I might be able to do this after all.*

"Complete conversations are about recognizing and repenting of all those negative pent up feelings we've had inside ourselves towards the other person," Suzanne said. "Those feelings emanate from us and the other person can feel them whether or not we actually speak them out loud. These feelings fill us with negative energy that interferes with our happiness."

"Now I want to invite you to participate in an activity that will strengthen your gift and ability to see the strengths and character traits in those around you," she said as she handed out a paper to each of us with an outline drawing of a person. "This drawing represents you and who you are becoming. We're going to write on these papers, but you won't be writing about yourself, you will be writing on everybody else's papers. Pair up and go from one person to another, looking into their eyes for a few seconds and see who they truly are, then write a word or a phrase of a quality that you recognize. After you've written on their paper then go to the next person and continue doing this until you've met with every person in the room. This is a silent activity. It will be done without talking to each other. It's not about what you say; this is about who you are."

YOU SPOT IT, YOU GOT IT

It was an interesting exercise. I had never done anything like that before. We walked from person to person, pausing long enough to spend a few seconds looking into their eyes until an impression came, then writing a word or phrase on their paper and moving on to the next person. After completing a circuit around the room, we returned to our seats.

"Now, take a moment to look at your paper and see the qualities that other people see in you," Suzanne said.

I read what the other ladies had seen when they looked into my eyes: beautiful, hopeful, gentle, pure in heart, loving, giving, happy and kind, genuine, caring, so strong, eternal progress, powerful leader and teacher. It was difficult not to start crying. How could they see those things in me when I couldn't perceive them in myself?

"Now I want you to think about the things that you wrote on everybody else's papers," Suzanne said. "Whatever traits you saw in others is because you also have that same quality within yourself, and that's why you recognize it. So on your paper, either mentally add all those qualities or actually write them down."

I wasn't expecting that and stopped to think about the qualities that I had seen in the other women and written on their papers. I saw a lot of love and compassion in them. Although each person was different, that was a recurring theme.

"The traits that we see in other people, whether good or bad, are things that we recognize because we have them ourselves. If you spot it, you got it," she said.

If you spot it, you got it? I mentally repeated and wrote it down in my notes.

"That means that if we are annoyed by certain traits, then we should be searching ourselves for those same behaviors,"

Suzanne continued. "If we're critical and annoyed with others, we would do well to look inside ourselves to see where we may be behaving in a similar way. If we're positive and at peace with the people around us, then that's a sign that we're in a good place ourselves. Remember, if you spot it, you got it."

"Okay, today so far we've discussed relationships, now we're going to talk about progression. Remember the three keys to happiness are identity, relationships, and progression," Suzanne continued.

Progression is what makes us feel fulfilled and happy.

"Progression is what makes us feel fulfilled and happy. The opposite of progression would be stagnation, or how about this word, 'damnation.' What do you think of when you hear that word?" Suzanne asked.

"Isn't that eternal punishment?," someone offered.

"You're right, but the word really means to stop progressing in the same way that a damn stops the flow of a river," she explained. "So using that word suggests that in our minds, the worst punishment we can think of is that we stop progressing."

I've never thought of it that way, I mused.

"Progression is a process of 'becoming,'" Suzanne said, "The goal is to become your best self and that requires change."

"We're going to talk about a couple more laws: the 'Law of Cause and Effect' and the 'Law of Gestation,'" she said. "The Law of Cause and Effect is related to an equal and opposite reaction, but in a way you may not have thought of before. As we make effort to reach what we want to become, then what we want to become also takes a step toward us. Likewise, when we take a step away from what we want to become, it also takes a step away from us. Therefore, don't despair if what you want seems far away, because it will move towards you as you progress, so that you only have to go half as far as you had imagined."

"The Law of Gestation refers to the natural law that there is a period of time between an action and the related result," Suzanne said. "Usually we use the word gestation to refer to pregnancy. We all know that it takes nine months gestation between the conception and the birth of a child. That same word could be used when we plant seeds in the garden. Usually packets of seeds will have information printed on the back of the package that tell how many days it takes from planting the seed until you can expect to have ripe produce to pick. Unfortunately, the healing process does not come with a printed label telling us how long it will take between the action and the result. We only know that there will be a period of time required for the effects to grow and mature. We simply have to keep going with the assurance that healing naturally takes time. That can be difficult when we're used to instant results. We get upset if it takes a few seconds for a program to download. We want an instant fix. Just know that's not going to happen. These things take time and there's really no way around that natural law."

We simply have to keep going with the assurance that healing naturally takes time.

"This line represents your path. It is a combination of your past experiences and actions and choices," she said as she drew a straight horizontal line on the board. "This point represents today," she said and drew a point at the right end of the line. "This is your point of power."

"Today you can choose to continue the same path that you have been traveling," she continued the horizontal line further, "or today you can choose to take another path."

She went back to the point on the line that represents today and began a different line slanting upwards from that point. "Today is the day for action. Your past does not determine your future. Your present determines your future."

"There is another law," she continued, "called the Law of

Perpetual Transmutation. That means the energy of the universe is always in a state of motion. It may change from one form to another, but it's always in motion and never standing still."

"We want to capitalize on this ability for energy to change form. Ideas that we create mentally or spiritually can come to reality. They do become reality. Have you ever heard the phrase 'as a man thinketh, so is he'? That isn't just a catchphrase; it is a reality," she said.

"We have things that we want in our lives and we either draw it to us or push it away by our thoughts. One tool that we can use to draw what we want towards us is through the creation of a vision board. A vision board is literally any sort of board on which you display images that represent whatever you want to be, do, or have in your life. This can be a powerful tool to help clarify, concentrate and maintain focus on a specific life goal. As I was preparing for this women's retreat, I placed a picture of this room on my vision board with a cluster of women gathering there. Twice a day I would focus on that image and then close my eyes, literally seeing the women come to fill the room."

Ideas that we create mentally or spiritually can come to reality. They do become reality.

"There are other tools as well," she continued. "Do you remember that I created an 'after story' for this retreat? I made an audio recording of what I wanted it to be like and listened to it every day. That was my mental or spiritual creation of this event which helped form the physical creation we're all enjoying this weekend."

"I am a mentor," Suzanne said, "I help people move through the process of creating goals and turning them into reality. Some of this is done through teaching, but a great deal of it is accomplished through a process called 'return and report.' Return and report is pretty much what it sounds like; I give assignments to my clients and they text me to let me know if they did it or not. There's no pressure or negativity; it simply creates a level of accountability and helps people stay on the path."

JAMIE

"It's time for our next guest speaker, who I'm so happy to have join us today. Jamie and I have been classmates in mentor training," Suzanne said. "She drove two hours to be here with us now since she had another appointment earlier today in another city."

"I had a plan for what I was going to teach today," Jamie began, "but during my drive today I had a distinct impression that I needed to change my presentation to share a certain story."

"It had rained recently and I was driving slowly through a dirt parking lot. It wasn't muddy and my tires didn't sink as I moved slowly along," she said as she drew a simple picture of a circle setting on a horizontal line to represent her tires going over the ground. "As I looked at the cars parked around me I noticed that each one had sunk slightly. You could even make a guess at how long various cars had been sitting in the same spot by the depth of the hole that the tires made," she drew another circle to represent a tire setting on a line with a pronounced dip in it where the tire rested. She turned away from her drawing to face us and asked a question, "Do you know what this kind of dip is called?"

"Is it a rut?" someone ventured.

"Not exactly, a rut is a long deep track made by the passage of wheels, and this is just a stationary dip," she explained. After a brief pause she continued while pointing to her figure on the board, "This is called a depression. A depression is caused by holding still and not moving forward. A depression is caused by a lack of progression."

Her words, though softly spoken, crashed over me like a wave. It felt as though her words were directed specifically to me. And they were. After the classes were done for the day, Jamie pulled me aside. "I didn't want to mention it in front of the whole group," she told me privately, "but when I got the impression to share this story, I also had the impression that it was for you."

Perhaps my depression was caused, or at least exacerbated, by my lack of progression. I felt that I failed at everything I attempted, so I stopped trying. I gave up trying to swim to shore and resigned myself to the task of merely treading water.

"Your past does not equal your future," she continued her presentation to the group. "Just because something has been a certain way does not mean it has to be that way in the future. What is your ideal for five years from now? What is the best it could be? What is your dream? What would you like your future to be like? I'm going to give you a few minutes to write your impressions."

What is your ideal for five years from now? What is the best it could be? What is your dream?

I wrote of happiness and rich relationships with my family. We're having a family dinner and everyone is gathered together and everyone gets along. I wrote about what I wanted for my children, about their happiness and success. I wrote about my dream backyard and how beautiful it is. It's a place where we want to gather. I wrote until I ran out of time.

Jamie pointed to the mountain view outside the window.

"These beautiful mountains weren't always this way. Mountains are formed as a result of the Earth's tectonic plates smashing together causing earthquakes and volcanoes. They are now peaceful and beautiful, stable and strong, but they were created in turmoil, upheaval, chaos and pain. Your past does not equal your future. The turmoil you currently face can be part of the creation of something beautiful, but we have to ask for it and we should be asking for the best."

I looked out the window at the mountain in front of me. I had never given thought to the idea that it wasn't always the majestic beauty that I saw before me. It had been created in turmoil. That was a powerful object lesson as I compared it to my own life. Could I really be peaceful and stable like a mountain? Its serenity and beauty now held a deeper meaning for me.

"What are some of the things that keep us from our goals?" she asked.

Together we made a list of obstacles including distractions, fear, pride, doubt, frustration, other people, failure, embarrassment, difficulty, uncomfortable, effort, takes too long, criticism, lack of support, etc.

"Okay, obstacles are going to happen, but I want you to learn to see them a different way," Jamie said. "Imagine that you're walking along a path and an obstacle drops in front of you. It doesn't have to be a wall that blocks you from your goal. If you climb over it, then it takes you a step higher. From your higher perspective you can see further and are closer to your goal. Reaching a goal is not like walking a straight path; it's like climbing a mountain and each obstacle you overcome is a step that raises you higher toward your goal."

Reaching a goal is not like walking a straight path; it's like climbing a mountain and each obstacle you overcome is a step that raises you higher toward your goal.

"I'm going to share a couple tools to get past obstacles," Jamie said. "The first is to to keep learning. As you continue to feed the mind and to feed the spirit it will help keep you from sinking into despair and depression. Another tool is to find a team of positive people with similar goals. These are people who help build you, these are not the people who tear you down."

"I mentor people as a group. I teach a new tool each week for six weeks and during that time my clients see incredible progress," she continued. "Gathering as a group is a powerful tool for healing and growth. This women's retreat is an example of that power. We are meeting in a group of like minded people in a positive environment with the goal of becoming better people. You are being strengthened and lifted by the awesome people around you."

"I want each of you to write a single goal," Jamie instructed. "A statement of what you want to be, but don't write it as if it's in the future, write it in the present tense beginning with the words, 'I am...'"

She gave us a few minutes to write a statement.

"Okay, now look at your statement and think of two specific actions that you can take each day to move yourself towards that goal," she said. "Remember these can be very small things like, smiling or speaking kindly, praying for someone, or having positive thoughts, but they must be specific actions that you can actually do."

She gave us a few minutes to write down our steps we would take towards becoming what we wanted.

"If you do those two small acts each day, you will be moving toward your goal and in turn your goal will be moving toward you," Jamie said. "It doesn't matter how fast you go. What matters is that you're moving forward. If you keep moving forward you'll get there."

It doesn't matter how fast you go. What matters is that you're moving forward.

"As a word of caution," she added, "do not mistake being busy with moving forward. Being busy doesn't do you any good. It's just treading water faster; it doesn't take you anywhere. Being busy is not the same as progression. So as you choose your actions, choose small and simple things that help you move forward."

Jamie wrapped up her presentation by having each of us take a turn mentioning one thing that impressed us from our lesson today and had us reteach that thing to the group.

Then came something that made my heart plummet.

Suzanne and Jamie each had made fliers for their services as mentors and handed them out. Each had special pricing available for participants in the retreat.

Oh, great, here comes the sales pitch, I thought.

I hate sales pitches. Every time someone brings up the topic of selling something, my defensive walls immediately rise and I retreat. I hate people asking for my money. It also makes me question everything that they've said. I don't trust that they want to help me; I figure that all they really want is my money and I don't want to give it to them.

I scanned skeptically through Jamie's flier first. She was offering two programs, one for adults and another for youth ages 12-18. They were group mentoring programs and like most classes, had a start date. The youth group class began in two months and the adult group class began in three months. The description read:

Join a phenomenal group of people as we work together to break out of ruts and move forward in amazing ways! It's your life. Make it shine!

- Gain tools to reduce negativity and increase positive thought
- Learn amazing, simple tools to improve your relationships and repair rifts
- Learn to become the person you want to be and love the person you already are
- Transform your connection with time and money from a burden to a blessing
- Learn how to make desired changes in your life easily and effectively
- Benefit from a live 60 minute online training each week
- Enjoy daily support and encouragement from this

phenomenal group of people as you progress!

A testimonial from a program participant read, "This 6 week course has seriously changed my life... I have grown so much during this course, and feel like I have taken leaps and bounds toward reaching my goals!"

I scanned the tuition price and wondered if this would be something that my teenage daughter would enjoy. I wished I could have brought her to the women's retreat. She would have enjoyed it. *She's the one person in my family who won't mock me for all of this,* I thought.

I scanned through Suzanne's flier. She listed prices for Body Code energy release sessions as well as three different mentoring packages. The one that interested me most was called the "Transformation Package." It was the most inclusive and, of course, was also the most expensive course she offered. It included:

- 3 month program with weekly sessions
- 6 bi-monthly 90 minute mentoring/Body Code sessions
- 5 bi-monthly 30 minute Body Code energy release sessions
- Daily accountability with 'return and report' contact

It also included the explanation that "weekly Body Code energy release helps you think and see things more clearly propelling you forward faster."

I thought about the price and pondered. I had some money saved in an account for my personal use and had enough saved to cover the cost of tuition. *Is this something that could help me?* I wondered. *I didn't want to spend money to come to this retreat.*

Actually I didn't want to come at all even if it had been offered for free, but I learned so many things and I'm truly glad that I came. I feel like the entire thing was organized just for me. There's no way that I'm going to be able to apply all this information on my own. I can't even remember most of what was said so there's no way I'm going to be able to apply it. I need someone to help me, and I don't think I'll get any support from home, but spending money for help bothers me. Is this a good thing or not?

Later I braved a conversation with Suzanne sharing my concern about spending money for information and help that I believed should be offered for free.

"You and I must be related," she laughed. "I felt exactly the same way. When I trained in the Body Code, I offered all my services for free. I had something valuable to help people and I wanted to help everybody as my service to humanity. My husband counselled me that I needed to charge so that people would value my service, but I ignored him. I figured that he was just upset at the money I had spent in training and wanted me to start earning instead of spending money."

I felt like the entire thing was organized just for me.

"The next year was one of the most miserable years of my life," she continued. "I worked myself ragged trying to help people who didn't appreciate my efforts at all. People would make appointments and I would rearrange my schedule to accommodate them and then they wouldn't show up. People would call and expect me to drop whatever I was doing and help them right now. People wouldn't follow up or let me know if I had helped them. I was overworked and underappreciated. I was miserable."

"I had to learn from my own experience that the advice my husband gave me was true," she said. "People need to make some kind of sacrifice in order to value something. Charging my clients isn't about me making money off them; it's about them making a tangible commitment and that's the only way they will apply what I have to offer. Since I started charging for my services, people value what I do. They follow through and that makes all the difference."

"I am no longer overworked and unappreciated," she continued. "I set my schedule and still have time for my family. People value my services and I know that I'm having a positive effect because my clients come back to me and let me know how much it has affected their lives. At this point I'm still spending more on training than I make on income, but someday those numbers may reverse and I'm okay with that. I'm making a difference for good and and my services are worth my price. I feel confident, happy, and appreciated now."

I never thought of it that way before, I pondered. *I'm not ready to make a decision yet, but I'm not as offended by the idea of hiring a mentor to help me.*

I tucked the fliers in with the rest of my notes for further consideration.

THE RETREAT - DAY 3

"Are you awake, too?" my mother asked.

"Yes, I haven't been sleeping very well lately," I replied.

It was about 4:00 a.m. and we had a hushed conversation in the dark.

"Are you going to read or try to go back to sleep?" my mother asked after a while.

"Actually, I was thinking about getting up. We've been talking about these 'complete conversation' things and I would like to give it a try and see if it does anything," I replied. "I'm hoping to find a quiet place where I can be alone. It's still quite dark outside, can I borrow the keys to your car and I'll go there until the sun comes up?"

She handed me the keys. "Good luck," she said.

"Thanks. I'll be back in time to prepare breakfast and I'll take my phone in case you need me," I said.

I quickly dressed and quietly made my way to the door, then headed to the underground parking garage and slid into the front seat of the car. I pulled out my notebook and flipped to the page where I had written my notes for how to have a 'complete conversation.'

One of these conversations was with my mother. I referred to my notes to begin.

"Okay, the first step is to invite the other person's higher self to talk with you," I read.

"Mom, can I please speak to your higher self, at the age you were when I was six years old," I began. I checked my notes for the next step, "Dump everything, holding nothing back, okay, here goes…"

"Mom, you chose not to love me," I began with tears welling in my eyes. "You chose not to be close to me. You made a choice. Do you have any idea what that choice did to me? Do you have any idea what it's like to grow up feeling like you're less than everybody around you? If your own mother doesn't love you, then you must be unlovable, unworthy of love. I have felt that way my entire life. I am worthless. I am nobody. These beliefs are my core identity. You healed over time, but I did not. I am still that broken unloved little girl. I needed you. I needed you to love me. I needed you to support me. I needed it like I needed air to breathe. I thought it was all my fault, that I had done something wrong. I thought there was something wrong with me..."

I have felt that way my entire life. I am worthless. I am nobody.

I continued the conversation until I couldn't think of anything else to say, then I checked my notes again for the next step.

"Apologize, ask the person to forgive you, and imagine them saying, 'Of course I forgive you,'" I read.

"Mom, I didn't understand it then, but now I know that you were hurting and were only trying to protect yourself. Even after I learned about the history and what happened and why, I didn't really understand. I didn't see how it was possible that a mother could do that to her child. It wasn't until I was crushed myself that I really understood what it must have been like for you. I get it now. I'm so sorry that you were hurt. I'm so sorry that you felt that you needed to build walls to protect yourself. I'm so sorry that I judged you. I'm so sorry that I've blamed you not only for things that were your fault but also for things that were really my own fault. Will you please forgive me?" I said.

Then I waited to 'hear' her higher self tell me, "Of course I do."

I took a deep breath before checking my notes again. Repeat this process with a conversation with God and again with yourself. I decided to break down my conversation with God into three separate conversations.

"Dear Heavenly Father, can I please speak to you?" I began, "Where were you? Isn't a father supposed to protect his children? How could you let this happen to me? I was just a child. I didn't understand. I didn't know what was happening and I blamed myself. Where were you when I needed you? Where are you now? I feel like my prayers are like buying a lottery ticket, I might get something good out of it, but chances are I will get nothing. It's a waste of my time. Yes, I've had a few prayers answered, but what about the thousands of prayers when I get nothing? It's not good enough that you're there occasionally. I need you to be there for me always. How can I trust you?..."

I continued the conversation until I couldn't think of anything else to say, then added, "I'm sorry for feeling that way. I probably don't understand the whole picture. Will you please forgive me?" I again waited a moment to 'hear' His response, "Of course I do."

"Dear Jesus Christ, can I please speak to you?" I began. I couldn't think of anything to dump on Him, so I simply said, "I'm sorry I didn't give this to you sooner. Will you please forgive me?"

I'm so sorry that you had to go through that. ... I'm so sorry for all you missed.

"Dear Holy Ghost, can I please speak to you?" I continued, "I'm sorry I have kept you from me. Will you please forgive me?"

I checked my notes again. The final step was to have a conversation with myself.

"Linda, can I please speak to your higher self when you were six years old?" I began. "Linda, you misunderstood everything and ruined your life. You have made your misery a self-fulfilling prophecy..." and I continued until I couldn't think of anything else to add.

"I'm so sorry that you had to go through that," I said. "I'm so sorry for all you missed. I'm so sorry that you were hurt, but it's time to let it go. Will you please forgive me? Will you forgive us? Let's move on."

I took a few deep breaths and did a quick self evaluation. How did I feel? I can't say that I felt 'lighter' since it wasn't akin to buoyancy; it was more like a plug had been removed and I was being drained. I was less heavy, but emotionally exhausted. I checked my watch. "I still have lots of time before the sun comes up; I'm going to keep going."

And I did. I had conversations with the people involved in my personal crushing earthquake, conversations with individuals, and conversations with groups of people. I had conversation after conversation for the next two and a half hours until the sun was up enough to go for a walk.

I took my notebook with me and walked along a mountain trail until I found a spot where I could sit and feel the warmth of the early morning sunshine on my face. I pulled out my notebook and searched for the page where I had taken notes on 'declarations.'

Okay, so I'm supposed to come up with at least five statements and repeat them three times. What should I say?

I didn't really know what to do except copy the ones that they had mentioned during the retreat. How about: I am loved, I know who I am, I love myself, my words have value, and I have the courage to speak my truth? I think those will do. Suzanne had instructed me to not just say the words, but to declare them like I meant them while doing actions, like spreading my arms wide or hugging them to myself as the words suggested. I felt pretty awkward and looked up and down the trail to make sure there weren't any other early morning hikers nearby to hear me make a fool of myself.

"I am loved!" I cried flinging my arms out wide.

"I know who I am!"

"I love myself!" I hugged my arms to myself.

"My words have value!" I spread my arms outward again.

"I have the courage to speak my truth!"

I didn't believe the words, but at least I could get them out. I looked up and down the trail again to check for clear before repeating the declarations a second and third time.

As I continued walking along the trail feeling pretty good about my efforts for the morning and feeling hope for the future, my phone rang. I thought it was my mother and checked my watch to see if I was late for breakfast preparation. It was my husband. My confidence failed entirely at the sound of his voice and I questioned everything that I had learned over the past two days.

"Good morning. How did you sleep?" he inquired.

"Not very well. I've been up for a while," I responded.

"What are you doing?" he asked.

"I, um, I just went for a sunrise hike this morning. It's really pretty up here…" I replied hesitantly. I was afraid that if he knew how I spent the past three hours he'd want to have me committed to a mental institution.

"Are you enjoying the retreat?" he asked.

"Yes, I'm learning a lot of great information," I said.

"Oh, good. What are you learning?" he asked.

"Um, well, there's a lot of information and I can't really sum it up very well." I evaded. "It's been like drinking out of a firehose."

After our brief conversation I thought, *I'm a fool. I'm not loved, I don't know who I am, I don't love myself, my words don't have any value, and I certainly don't have the courage to speak my truth.*

I took a deep breath and walked back to the condo to begin making breakfast.

PAINTING

The third and final day was only a half day of lessons and included a group project of painting a picture together.

Suzanne introduced the guest speaker for the day, who happened to be our mother.

"We've been talking about the three keys of happiness: identity, relationships, and progression," Suzanne began. "My mother is the epitome of progression. She has been learning and progressing her entire life. She raised her family while continuing to develop her own musical talents. She has taught hundreds of students piano lessons and voice lessons over several decades. After her children were raised, she went back to school and pursued her various interests. She learned about color analysis, makeup and acrylic nails. She studied herbology. She went to midwifery school and certified as a doula, which is training to assist and support another woman during childbirth so that she could provide skilled help and support as her last grandchildren were born. She went back to school to learn computer skills and became certified as a travel agent. Over the past several years, she has been developing her artistic talents and has taken classes at the community college as well as taking private lessons. She has had her artwork in several art shows and has a growing collection of prize ribbons."

Listening to Suzanne talk about my mother was like hearing about her for the first time. I never realized how amazing she was because I was too busy feeling hurt and resentful. My new appreciation continued to grow when my mother displayed a few of her paintings and I heard the 'oohs' and 'aahs' from the ladies around me.

My mother's presentation topic was 'How you fit in the big picture, you matter.' I'm not sure what the other women heard, but to hear my mother say that 'I matter' meant a great deal to me, because I have never felt like I mattered to anyone, and I especially wanted to matter to her.

She led a general discussion of talents and skills and eventually tied it into the topic of painting. One thing that stands out was the discussion on complementary colors. She drew the standard color wheel with the primary and secondary colors in their interconnected circular order: red, orange, yellow, green, blue, and purple.

"Complementary colors are the colors that are opposite to each other on the color wheel," she explained. "Red and green are complementary colors, as are yellow and purple, and orange and blue. The high contrast of complementary colors create a vibrant look."

"The word complementary, is derived from the root word 'complete,'" she continued. "When things are complementary they are combined in such a way as to enhance or emphasize the qualities of each other. Synonyms for complementary include the words harmonious, compatible and corresponding."

It brought to mind our earlier lesson on energy types and my question about why we tend to seek our opposite in a spouse.

Perhaps because we are opposite we complete each other? I thought. *Maybe at some subconscious level, we seek what we lack so that we can be complete? These are ideas worth pondering.*

It was strange to think of opposite as meaning harmonious, compatible and corresponding. I tend to think of opposite as a basis for conflict.

"In our lives we have opposition," my mother continued. "Opposition completes us. It helps us progress and strengthens us. It brings out talents and abilities we didn't know we had. Opposition is necessary for growth. Opposition highlights the good things we have. Nothing makes us appreciate health like being sick. Nothing helps us appreciate freedom like imprisonment. Nothing makes us appreciate light like being in the dark. Feeling despair enables us to appreciate joy. Feeling sadness enables us to appreciate happiness. These things are difficult, but it will all work out in the end. That means that if it hasn't worked out yet, then it's not the end."

Interesting thought, I mused. *I guess I'm not at the end. It certainly hasn't worked out yet, so I must be in the middle somewhere. I hope to not always be in the middle. Is there really an end somewhere? Could there really be an end to sadness, hopelessness and despair?*

I wasn't sure, but I hoped it could be possible.

She showed a painting of a colorful sunset reflected on a body of water. On a separate canvas, she had sketched the outline of that same picture and we were each to take part in painting this new picture. One by one we approached the canvas and took our turn with the paintbrush as she instructed us where to apply the color.

When I had heard that this would be a part of the retreat, I panicked. I didn't have an artistic bone in my body. I could paint walls with a roller and a brush; that was the extent of my painting abilities. I was terrified that whatever I did to the painting would surely ruin it. Thus when it was my turn to approach the painting, I did so with trepidation. My color was orange. I had two turns, one to paint the orange in the sky and a second turn to paint the corresponding orange reflected in the water.

I panicked. I didn't have an artistic bone in my body.

When my second turn was completed I was both relieved that I was done and pleased that my contribution hadn't ruined the overall effect.

Then when everyone had taken their turns, I was called back to complete the painting with a wavy yellow line of the sun reflecting in the water. It was central to the painting and I was terrified, but did as I was instructed; when I stepped back to see the overall effect, I liked it. I liked the painting very much and my contribution hadn't ruined the scene, but had added to its beauty. The painting was set aside to dry and I found myself glancing at it from time to time and admiring it.

I can't believe I helped create that. It's good and I'd really like to have it, I thought.

"So who gets the painting?" I nonchalantly asked my mom. "Are you going to give it to Suzanne to remind her of the retreat she organized? I bet she'd really appreciate that." I said, fully expecting the answer to be yes.

I can't believe I helped create that.

"No, she didn't ask for it. Actually, I was thinking about giving it to you. Would you like to have it?" she replied.

"Yes, thank you. I would like that very much," I smiled and hugged her. Now it wasn't just a painting. It was my painting, and it was something good that I helped to create.

Now the retreat was over. It was time to pack up and return home. I had not wanted to come, but now that it was over, I was afraid to go home. During these past three days, I had learned so much and had a beginning of hope that I could change and improve my reality. However, it hadn't performed a magical and instant transformation.

If this works at all, it's still going to take a long time. I worried. *If my family, particularly my husband, doesn't see immediate results, I don't think they'll support me in this at all. They'll think it's weird. They'll make fun of me and may even try to stop me. I'm so scared of what they'll say. I think the things I've learned are true principles, they feel right, but I don't have the confidence to defend myself and I don't really know enough to explain this stuff, anyway.*

One thing I knew was that I was going to need help; there's no way I could make this transformation on my own. I couldn't even remember most of what we talked about. There was so much information that I felt overwhelmed. I couldn't make all those changes at once.

I need to start small with maybe one or two things and I need a mentor, someone who will support me on my journey, I thought.

I reread the fliers that Suzanne and Jamie had handed out the day before. Jamie's group mentoring class didn't start for another three months, and I wanted to start now. Suzanne's individual mentoring could start at any time and lasted three months.

Huh, I thought, *I guess I could really do both. I can start Suzanne's now and it should be finished by the time Jamie's begins.*

I started writing checks right then, while I still had the courage to commit, because I knew that my courage would fade once I returned home. I also scheduled my initial appointment with Suzanne for the following week.

I'm going to do this. I committed, then packed my bags and headed home.

THE BEGINNING

"Welcome home!"

My family welcomed me with hugs and smiles.

"I missed you," my husband said. "Home is not the same without you."

"Thanks," I replied. "It's good to be back."

They wanted to hear all about the retreat and I referred to my notes sharing all the parts that I thought they'd like while concealing all the parts that I thought they'd reject.

"It was awesome. I'm really glad I went," I said. "I realized that I've lost my voice, and I'd like to try to get it back," I dared to add. I was relieved when no one mocked or criticized me for my declaration. My shoulders relaxed a little.

This is going to be okay, I thought, or at least hoped.

One unexpected downside of attending the retreat was that now my mom was aware of my secret struggle with depression and also informed my father. Now they wanted to 'fix' me, too. They visited often with a look of expectation in their eyes that I would flip on a switch and suddenly be all better.

At this point, I didn't know what works to overcome depression, but I did know a few things that did not work.

Telling me that I shouldn't be depressed didn't help.

Reminding me of all the wonderful things I should be grateful for and that I had no reason to be depressed didn't help. My problem was not that I was blind or that I had lost my memory.

Telling me how wonderful I was and trying to build me up was the worst thing of all. Compliments were excruciatingly painful. My mind rejected them as lies. I thought that either you were lying to me, or you were making fun of me, or that you were deceived by my playacting and that if you only knew the truth you would see that I was a fraud.

I endured their well-meaning visits with polite detachment and wondered if letting my secret slip out had been a big mistake.

My first mentoring appointment wasn't until the following week, but I didn't want to lose the momentum from the retreat. I wanted to get started right away, so I tried to do some of the things that I could remember from the lessons on my own. I continued with the declarations each morning and had a few more complete conversations, but I couldn't think of anyone else I needed to 'talk' to.

I thought I'd try the 'scripture instant messaging' that Suzanne had taught. The first step was to choose an inspired religious text like the Bible, Torah or Quran to read. Although we may understand the nature of God differently, He knows we're all speaking to the same being, whether we recognize it or not. I chose a religious text from the scriptural canon of The Church of Jesus Christ of Latter Day Saints called The Book of Mormon. I loved it because it speaks so clearly and was easy to understand.

I downloaded the free LDS Gospel Library app onto my phone which also included a notebook tool that I could use to write my notes, and turned to a random chapter. I opened the notebook tool and wrote, "What am I supposed to do next? How do I heal? How do I get happy?", said a prayer and hoped that this experiment would give me some answers.

What am I supposed to do next? How do I heal? How do I get happy?

I was blown away as I read through the chapter. The answers started coming in the very first verse. I paused and wrote the answers and impressions that came to my mind in the notebook tool. I read the next verse and stopped again to write in the notebook the thoughts and impressions that came. I was going along well until a verse made me stop and think. It said, "..the Lord was with thee; and thou knowest that the Lord did deliver thee." I felt like it applied to me somehow, but I couldn't figure out how since it was phrased in the past tense and I was asking for help now.

I'm not healed yet. What does it mean by 'did deliver thee'? I wondered. I pondered until the memory resurfaced of the day I was sobbing in the car on the way home from dropping my daughter off at school. I had asked for help and had felt a measure of calmness comfort me.

Well, what do you know. I guess He did deliver me, I thought. I wrote about the experience in my notes. Perhaps I hadn't been as abandoned as I thought. I felt my anger towards God abate ever so slightly.

When I finished reading through the chapter I went back and reread all the notes I had written. There was a note written after nearly every verse. Messages of peace, of comfort, assurance of God's confidence in me, counsel about the law of the harvest, counsel to keep God's commandments and to trust in Him, counsel to move forward and act, a warning to watch out for pride and boasting in my own strength. It was as if this chapter was included just to speak to me personally, and yet as I reread it without the template of my question in mind, it was just an account of a father giving counsel to his son.

I had asked for help and had felt a measure of calmness to comfort me.

The following day, filled with the confidence of yesterday's success, I tried the scripture instant messaging again turning to the following chapter and writing my next question in my notebook tool, "I am supposed to be setting goals. What do I need most? What should I be seeking? What should I be changing?" I said a prayer and began to read.

The chapter began with, "And now, my [daughter Linda], I have somewhat more to say unto thee…"

As I read through searching for answers, the verses opened

to me, but this time rather than words of comfort and praise, it pointed out my faults and the need to change and repent. When I finished the chapter and read through my notes I found that I had written, "This chastisement is for my good. I can't hide my crimes from God and need to acknowledge my faults. I have boasted in my own strength and wisdom. I need to be nourished by others and give heed to their counsel," and many more things.

While not nearly as satisfying as yesterday's encouraging chapter, since it brought to mind my faults, it still felt as if it were speaking directly to me. I did ask what I needed to change. Did I expect it to be told, "You don't need to change a thing; you're perfect just the way you are"? I pondered over my notes throughout the day.

The third day, I tried again, turning to the following chapter, and wrote in my notebook the question of my heart.

"I'm trying, but it's so hard. Harder than I imagined. I'm afraid of failing. Afraid that it won't work or won't be worth it. Is it worth it? Will you help me?"

I said a prayer and began to read.

The chapter began with, "Now my [daughter, Linda] … I perceive that thy mind is worried…"

As I read through the chapter I didn't stop after nearly every verse to write a note. I didn't see anything that applied to me at all after that one statement in the first verse. Disappointed, I reread it and searched again. In this rereading I still didn't see anything that seemed to apply to me, but I did notice repetitions and patterns in themes and highlighted those. One phrase that was repeated often was simply "God knoweth." I reread the chapter a third time, this time without the template of my question, to see what the chapter was talking about. After reading through the third time, I finally had my answer and wrote the following in my notes:

"The man speaking, named Alma, inquired diligently and learned some things, but even in that one thing, he wasn't told everything. He had to continue on in faith and trust that God knows and that it will be okay. Sigh. Not the answer that I was hoping for. The answer is 'Be still and know that I am God.'"

The following day, I was much more hesitant to try the scripture instant messaging experiment again, but I was bothered by something and desperately wanted guidance.

The thing that bothered me was a feeling, an impression, that came to my mind that I needed to write my experiences and share them. The thought filled me with horror.

Me, the person who hides in the back of the room to make a quick escape before anybody asks the dreaded question, 'how are you?' because I have so much to to hide? Me, the person who is filled with internal turmoil and feels like a fraud, I'm supposed to write my experience and bear the secrets of my soul to share with anybody who will listen? What a horrible thought. Where did it come from?

Filled with trepidation, I turned to the following chapter and wrote in the notebook tool.

"I feel like I received inspiration and direction this morning. I want to move forward in faith, but I've been deceived before and I'm scared. How do I move forward in faith?"

I read through the chapter and saw absolutely nothing that applied to me. I read through a second time and again saw nothing. My confidence shattered, I questioned everything that I thought I had learned in the past few days. Was it all in my mind? Had I made up the whole thing? I was so disappointed. My deception, if it was a deception, had been a beautiful thing. How I wished that it was real, that I could ask of God and He would hear me and give me answers. How can I find the words to describe the thoughts and disappointments of my heart?

Dejectedly, I read through the chapter again, hoping against hope that there would be something that would validate the previous days' experiences. In this reading, although I didn't see anything that pertained to me or to my question, I did notice a pattern. A certain word was repeated over and over. It was a strange word: 'requisite.' *What does requisite even mean?* I wondered.

I looked it up in a dictionary, sat back and pondered. Then I wrote in my notebook tool, "Requisite means a thing that is necessary for the achievement of a specified end—how does this apply to my question? Moving forward is requisite. There is no other way."

It was not the answer I was hoping for, but it was the reason that I began writing this journal. I had no assurance of how my story would turn out. I had no assurance of how it would be received by others. All I knew was that it was 'requisite' that I do it, and so I wrote.

I didn't try the 'scripture instant messaging' again. I didn't think I had a right to ask any more questions until I had acted on what I already received.

THE FIRST MENTORING SESSION

Finally the day of my first appointment arrived and I made the forty-five minute drive to my sister Suzanne's house. I was nervous. I don't like asking people for help. Somehow needing other people makes me feel like I'm a failure because I couldn't do it on my own.

Suzanne had emailed me a questionnaire a few days before with instructions to fill it out and email it back to her before our first appointment.

"I need to know where you're at and what you want so that I can tailor the session for your specific goals," she said.

I was embarrassed as I filled out the questionnaire, feeling exposed and naked as I answered the questions. It felt like a confession of my weaknesses that I've worked so hard to hide for a very long time, but I did it and braced myself for her reaction.

Suzanne welcomed me with a hug and ushered me into her office.

"I read through your questionnaire and we have a lot of things to work on, but I think the best place to start is with recovering your voice," she began. "After you change and regain your confidence a lot of other things will fall into place. You'll notice that people will treat you differently and your relationships will automatically improve."

"I'm going to give you a homework assignment, but first I'm going to teach you a lesson and I want you to take good notes, because you will be teaching it back to me so I know that you really understand the concept," she said.

She drew two vertical lines on a page to separate the paper into three columns. The first she labeled "Has Been," the middle column was labeled "Is," and the final column was labeled "Will Be." She drew a stick figure in the center column.

"Okay," she began, "this is where you are today. This little figure represents you."

She drew a horizontal line from the stick figure that traversed into the column labeled "Will Be" and continued, "This line represents the path to take you from where you are to where you want to go. These little tick marks that I'm drawing along your path represent action steps that are necessary to progress along that path. However you'll notice that there is a wall between where you are and where you want to be," she pointed to the line separating the columns.

"You are going to hit this wall and it's going to be uncomfortable. I want to explain what that wall is, how it got there, and how to move past it," she said.

"The wall is created by your subconscious. Your subconscious is a set of automatic programs that are designed to protect you and keep you safe, they create your 'comfort zone.' However these programs are often faulty and need to be reprogramed. When you try to step beyond that comfort zone you will hit this wall and your subconscious will work very hard to tell you to come back because you are traveling to a place that is unsafe, unfamiliar, uncomfortable, and unpredictable. It will tell you that what you believe to be on the other side of that wall is a lie."

You are going to hit this wall and it's going to be uncomfortable.

"The subconscious built this wall based on the evidence of past experience. You've already experienced this and even mentioned on your questionnaire 'once burned twice shy' as one of the reasons for your current state of feeling unsafe," she went on. "The evidence of past experience, regardless of how miserable it may actually be is considered 'safe' because it is familiar, predictable, and comfortable. What has been is considered 'truth' by your subconscious and what you want is considered a 'lie'. As you work toward your goal and hit that wall, your subconscious will try to protect you by telling you to come back to where it's safe. Does that make sense?"

I nodded.

"Okay, the only way to get past this wall is by continuing to take those action steps towards your goal. As you take those new action steps, it will create new evidence that your subconscious can assimilate. What was once unfamiliar and uncomfortable will become familiar and comfortable and your subconscious can reprogram itself with this new evidence of what is 'safe.'" she said. "If you keep going you can get past this wall," she promised.

The only way to get past this wall is by continuing to take those action steps towards your goal.

"However, if you stop and turn back when it gets uncomfortable you will only validate and add to the stockpile of subconscious evidence that insists that this wall which keeps you from reaching your goal is necessary for your safety," she warned.

"It will actually strengthen that wall and make it more difficult to transverse in future attempts. You mentioned in your questionnaire that you have a tendency to start things and not finish them," she added. "That is probably because you hit this wall and your subconscious told you to stop and go back to where it was safe. Okay, now teach me this concept that I just explained," she instructed.

I explained about the wall, where it came from and how to get past it, feeling confident in my understanding of the concept.

"Very good," she said. "Now let's move on."

She drew a cartoon outline of a person. "Do you remember how we talked about the positive and negative energy balance at the retreat?"

"Yes," I replied.

"Good," she said. "So you know that we have positive and

negative energy in our bodies," she said as she drew little plus signs and negative signs inside the cartoon drawing. "And the goal is to remove negative and add more positive."

"Yes, I remember that," I said.

"Excellent," she said. She then drew a circle divided in half by a horizontal line. On the top half she wrote the word 'conscious' and in the bottom half she wrote the word, 'subconscious.' "Okay, do you also remember how we talked about the conscious and subconscious parts of our mind?" she said.

"Yes," I replied.

"Good," she said. "This line between the conscious and subconscious represents a filter that exists between them. When we hear things that we don't believe or that aren't safe they enter the conscious mind hit that filter and bounce right back out again. They never enter the subconscious because they are rejected. This can be a problem when we say our declarations because they are things that our subconscious rejects as being lies and it doesn't have a lot of effect. They're still good and eventually will get through but it takes a long time."

"Music, however," she said, "gets through that filter and enters the subconscious much quicker. Music is an incredibly powerful tool to help reprogram our subconscious and reset that filter. Got it? Okay now teach this back to me," she instructed.

I explained the concepts back to her as I understood them.

"Good," she said, "So for your assignment this week I want you to choose three songs with positive lyrics. These must be songs that speak to you and mean something to you. I want you to print out a copy of the lyrics and email them to me by Wednesday at noon."

Okay, I thought. *So far so good. I can do that.*

"Then you're going to sing these songs out loud. Sing all the words and sing it as if it's talking to you. Sing one song each day, rotating through the three songs. I also need you to send me a recording of you singing one of those songs by Friday at noon," she instructed.

Panic set in.

"Um, not only is that terrifying because I have a 'choir' voice, not a 'solo' type voice, but I don't know how to send a recording of a song," I replied.

She taught me how to download a phone app to record my voice and then send it as a text. Dang.

"Okay," she said, "you can choose any songs you'd like. I thought of a song that might work for you. It's called 'Brave' by Sara Bareilles."

"Oh, I love that song," I said.

"Good," she replied, "Here is a copy of the lyrics. We're going to sing it together now."

BRAVE

My panic and embarrassment heightened, but I stood by her as she held up the lyrics and turned on the music.

Everybody's been there, everybody's been
Stared down by the enemy
Fallen for the fear and done some disappearing
Bow down to the mighty
Don't run, stop holding your tongue
Maybe there's a way out of the cage where you live
Maybe one of these days you can let the light in
Show me how big your brave is

Say what you wanna say
And let the words fall out
Honestly I wanna see you be brave...

I've heard the song many times, but the only words I really understood were in the chorus. As I read and sang the words with my sister I couldn't believe how well they matched my story. Tears streamed down my face and there were a couple times when I couldn't even get through the words, I just sobbed instead. Even though I sounded horrible, that was a pretty powerful experience.

After we finished the song, she gave me the rest of my assignment for the next two weeks until the next mentoring session. She gave me two tracking sheets. One was an action step tracking form with four columns. The first column was for the date, the second was for the action step, in my case singing a song, and the third and fourth columns simply said 'did' and 'did not.'

"Each day you record the date and the action step and either mark the column saying that you either did it or did not do it. Every night you'll take a picture of this form and text it to me. Do you know how to send a picture on your phone?" she asked.

"Yes, I can do that," I replied.

"Good." She went on. "Now on this second form you record two successes and accomplishments that you did each day. I only need to see this form once a week. Take a picture of it and text it to me on Friday night or Saturday morning."

"Okay, I think I got it," I said, marking each sheet with the appropriate instructions.

When I got home, I immediately started researching song lyrics to see which three I should choose. I definitely wanted "Brave" by Sara Bareilles. After reading through the lyrics to several songs, I decided to choose "Try Everything" by Shakira and "Roar" by Katy Perry as the other two. I printed off the lyrics and emailed a copy to Suzanne. I was feeling pretty good about the progress of the day until I hit that emotional wall that Suzanne had warned me about.

One of my grown daughters was visiting and had asked about my mentoring session. I pulled out my notes and was explaining what I'd learned. Then suddenly my husband interrupted us to ask a question.

"Just a minute Dad," my daughter said, "Mom is teaching me about her 'hoogie poogie.'"

I froze. *I can't believe she just used that term, and in front of Lewis, too,* I thought. *She's not interested in what I'm learning. She's making fun of me.*

To my husband's credit, he defended me by saying, "Whatever she's doing seems to be making a difference. I think it's a good thing."

Although I appreciated his supportive words, they weren't enough to mend the tear in my soul. Even as it was happening, the logical side of me recognized that my mountain response didn't match the molehill offense, but my emotions were overpowering. It literally felt like my life and my very existence were being threatened.

I don't have words to adequately convey how badly that hurt. I had lost my voice. I usually stayed silent because I was afraid that no one cared what I think, anyway, or that they would mock me. I had taken the risk to speak up and share something that was important to me and my fears were once again validated. It was as if I had removed my armor and exposed the tender flesh only to have it flayed from my bones. I excused myself and went to my room, where I sobbed hysterically.

I don't have words to adequately convey how badly that hurt.

I can't do this! I'm not safe! It's all a lie! I cried. *My words will never have value. No one will ever value me. I need my walls to protect me. I have to turn back.*

I had thought that I understood the lesson about the subconscious building a wall to protect me from moving forward, but I had no idea how very real that wall was.

I remembered my assignment to sing a song, so I pulled out my printed lyrics and played the song on my phone while I sobbed my way through "Try Everything" by Shakira.

I messed up tonight
I lost another fight
I still mess up but I'll just start again
I keep falling down
I keep on hitting the ground
I always get up now to see what's next

Birds don't just fly
They fall down and get up
Nobody learns without getting it wrong

I won't give up, no I won't give in
Till I reach the end
And then I'll start again
Though I'm on the lead
I wanna try everything
I wanna try even though I could fail...

After singing it through three times, I felt calm enough to function again. I knew my response had hurt my daughter's feelings and I felt terrible about that. She had written a sweet apology note which I found tucked in my mentoring notes, and although I appreciated the effort, I also didn't believe a word of it. It was so much easier to believe negative than positive. I gave her a hug, "I'm so sorry. I don't have very thick skin right now," I said.

Before going to bed, I filled in my personal tracking form and texted a picture to Suzanne. I made it through the first day. I had no idea it would be this hard.

I wasn't in a deep depression, but it wasn't good, either.

The rest of the week was a mixed bag. I wasn't in a deep depression, but it wasn't good, either. I tried to speak up a few times, but my ideas were shot down and questioned. I hosted a small party, which was always terrifying to me because I was afraid no one would show up. It wasn't very well attended, but those who did come had a great time and didn't want to leave, so I wasn't sure if it was a failure because some people didn't come, or if it was a success because those who did come really enjoyed it.

Another day I was at an extended family gathering and all I wanted to do was escape. It took a lot of effort to engage in polite conversation. I endured for long enough to hopefully be inconspicuous before I made my escape. I tried to keep it together, but I could feel the tears welling up inside.

I have kept the tears at bay for five days now. I survived another day, I thought. *I just want to give up. Sticking my neck out is too painful. I want to retreat to where it's safe.*

However, I continued to say my morning 'declarations,' sing my song, write two successes, fill out my tracking forms, and return and report each day.

TRAPPED EMOTIONS

After a week it was time to meet with Suzanne again. This time wasn't a mentoring session, just a Body Code session for releasing trapped emotions.

As she worked on me, the experience of me as a six year-old little girl kept coming up. She removed emotions such as: abandonment, shock, forlorn, confusion, betrayal, longing, etc., but the one that stopped her in her tracks was the emotion 'shame.'

"Why would you feel shame?" She inquired. "You certainly didn't do anything wrong."

Tears rolled down my cheeks again as memories flooded back.

"Because there's something wrong with me. I couldn't make her love me." I said.

"Oh, you blamed yourself. I see," she said. "That's so sad."

So that's where it comes from, I thought, *I often feel ashamed even though I've done nothing wrong. I'm simply ashamed of my very existence. I'm ashamed that I'm me, a worthless, useless, unlovable being.*

"You're the water energy type, right?" she asked.

I nodded.

"Water energy type are motivated by relationships," she said. "That's probably why this affected you so very deeply. Also you were very young. Children take things very literally. Your interpretation that nobody loved you became your reality. I was thirteen when Becky married and moved away, I understood better what was going on, and since I'm the earth energy type, my thoughts went right to 'fix it' mode. That has been my struggle; I thought it was my job to fix everything and make everybody happy."

"That sounds like a good thing," I said.

"It isn't. I don't have any power over another person's happiness," she said. "I've been fighting a losing battle my whole life and have always felt like a failure. In my declarations I had to say 'I trust that other people are capable of making their own decisions about life' and things like that. It's been a challenge to let go and not try to rescue all the people I love. It has been so freeing to finally let go of that burden."

"I never knew that this affected you as well," I said. "You always looked so strong and perfect."

"It just affected us differently, that's all," she replied. "Mom is a water energy type, too," she continued. "She thrived on her relationship with Becky; perhaps that's why her leaving affected Mom so deeply."

"What are you saying for your declarations?" she asked.

"'I am loved', 'I know who I am', 'I love myself', 'my words have value', and 'I have the courage to speak my truth,'" I replied.

"Okay, those are good, but I want you to add another one, you need to say 'my mother loves me,' as well. This has been a huge issue in your life," she said. "Have you had a complete conversation with Mom?"

"Yes," I replied.

"Have you also had one with your six year-old self?" she asked.

"Yes," I replied.

"Excellent," she said. "It's probably going to take more than one. It may take several. You need to allow yourself to feel it and validate those feelings so you can let them go. Also, have conversations with all the rest of the family members. You've felt neglected and unimportant to all of us. It makes me sad you've gone through all this. Here you thought no one cared about you and all I was thinking at the time was that you were a cute little girl."

After we finished my mind was in a whirl.

It's not just Mom that I thought didn't love me; it's my whole family. It's not just one person that I have issues with; it's the whole world. I thought. I have always felt that I'm not important to anyone, but to say the words out loud sounds strange and unnerving. How is it possible to know something and not know it at the same time? I can't imagine a reality where I don't feel worthless, unimportant and unloveable.

It may sound strange, but the possibility of a new reality frightened me. I felt safer in my familiar world where at least I knew what to expect.

Another day I recorded in my journal, "I failed again today. I'm tired of rejection. I don't feel 'lighter'; I feel drained. Memories and thoughts are surfacing that I completely forgot about. These are issues that I've buried long ago and hoped that they'd simply gone away. They hadn't. It's unsettling and scary even. I hope there's something better on the other side or else this is definitely not worth it."

I failed again today. I'm tired of rejection.

About two weeks after the initial appointment, my husband and I had an adventure going canoeing down the Jordan River together. It was beautiful. We saw a blue heron, a pelican, scores of baby ducklings and goslings with their protective mothers, and hundreds of swallows emerging from their mud caves in a flurry of animated flight, filling the air with the beating of wings and the sound of their cries. It was magical. We enjoyed the scenery and joked playfully.

"I love being able to banter with you," my husband said. "I've missed you."

His words surprised me. He was right. I was different today. When was the last time I felt joy or appreciated beauty? When was the last time I could joke or laugh? I haven't noticed because it had been gradual, but I was feeling happy more often.

The following day I had two social events on the same day. The first one was a surprise birthday party for a friend. I was impressed at the effort her husband and family had put into the event. They had totally succeeded in keeping it a secret and my friend was completely caught by surprise. The house was crowded with people and good food. All the guests signed a giant birthday banner and wrote birthday wishes. It was a lovely party and I was happy for my friend; however, I was also struggling with jealous thoughts. No one would ever do anything like this for me, I thought. And even if I took the time to organize it, no one would show up for a party meant to honor me. I was able to endure it without falling apart and engaged in polite conversation before I left early to brace myself for the second social event for the evening.

I have been in a book club with a wonderful group of women for over a decade. We meet monthly to discuss a book and just to socialize. I used to love it, and I still love the people, but it's even harder to hide from friends than it is to hide from strangers. It takes a tremendous amount of effort to keep up pretenses and a lot of effort to steer conversations away from myself towards other people with less to hide. That night, I was able to actively participate in conversation and didn't want to run away, and furthermore, I did it on a rebound from struggling through the first event of the evening. I was pretty proud of myself for that accomplishment, which would be minor for some, but monumental for me.

It's even harder to hide from friends than it is to hide from strangers.

On my personal tracking sheet, I was able to record my success that night. I survived two social events in a single day.

We needed to postpone my next mentoring session since Suzanne was out of town. I wanted to continue the pattern of weekly Body Code sessions so I scheduled an appointment with my acupuncturist. Often when a particular emotion and associated age are brought up, I can immediately identify the event that occurred and memories resurface, but sometimes nothing comes to mind. I can't think of anything in particular that happened and it's a bit confusing.

"There are feelings of helplessness from five years ago," he said.

"I know exactly what that is," I said and a few tears escaped my eyes as the horrible memory of past events were brought to the forefront of my mind and my feelings of utter helplessness. I could not stop the events from happening, nor did I have any power to repair the consequences. It was awful.

I was baffled. I couldn't think of any major event that occured at that time.

"Let's let that one go," he said reassuringly and released the trapped emotion. Then he found a trapped emotion that I couldn't identify an event to go with it. It was something to do with feelings about my role as a wife and it occurred somewhere around the age of 27. I was baffled. I couldn't think of any major event that occurred at that time. He said that sometimes things will come up without a major event, but are things that we need to be made aware of so that we can deal with them.

When we finished the session and I went home, I was still bothered by the memories and feelings that had resurfaced. I remembered the object lesson that Suzanne had done with the ping pong balls in the water pitcher. I hate these stupid ping pong balls surfacing. They hurt. I had buried them so deep, I forgot they existed. *I don't like having to deal with them,* I thought.

Soon afterwards, I had a lunch date with my husband. I picked him up during his lunch break from work and we tried a new restaurant. He was delighted that I had made the effort to come and make this happen and I think he had a good time, but

I felt an unidentifiable anger welling up inside me that marred the experience for me. On the drive home I had my first yelling, swearing complete conversation. I did not know that those words were inside me. I felt rather like a two year-old having a temper tantrum. It made no logical sense, but there was a lot of anger and frustration inside that needed to get out. It was kind of a rough day and I felt drained and confused.

The following day I had two more social events: a bridal shower for a friend and a birthday party for my husband's aunt who was celebrating her eigthieth birthday. For a long time, I had to brace myself for social events and put on a good face to endure them, but on this day I was animated and actively engaged. I laughed and joked and had a great time. *I can't remember the last time I actually enjoyed a social function, and today I had two and enjoyed them both. I feel good. I see glimpses of who I used to be,* I thought. *I could get used to this.*

THE SECOND MENTORING SESSION

It was finally time for the second mentoring session. Suzanne had sent another pre-visit questionnaire which I filled out and she reviewed to monitor my progression. I had had a few good days and lots of bad days, so I wasn't sure how to answer the questions. My answers could be very different depending on the day.

"This is an interesting answer," she said. "Where the question says, 'write one word to describe yourself' you wrote 'hesitant'. Is there a story behind that?"

"I don't know. Sometimes I'm doing fine and other times I'm struggling," I explained. "I'm trying to move forward, but sometimes I want to go back."

"From reading through your questionnaire, I think the things you're struggling with the most right now are insecurity and comparing yourself with others," she said. "Does that sound right to you?"

"Definitely," I responded.

"Okay," she continued. "Insecurity comes from having a low energy balance."

She drew the familiar outline figure of a person and drew plus signs and minus signs on it.

"Do you remember our conversations about energy balance?"

"Yes," I replied.

"When you have a low energy balance with too many negatives and not enough positives you feel insecure. You become paralyzed by fear," she said. "What we want is a high energy balance. A high energy balance leads to security. We want lots of positives. You need to nurture yourself. Make sure you get enough rest, spend time in nature, and do nice things for yourself."

"You need to get rid of negative and add positive," she repeated. "You've been singing and that adds positive. Make it a habit. I'm going to give you new assignments this time, but don't stop the singing. Is singing becoming easier?"

"Yes," I replied. "I can get through the songs pretty easily now."

"That's good," she replied. "You may want to pick new songs. When the words to a song no longer make you cry, you might need something else that speaks to you. Crying is actually a good thing. It is a release. It helps take out the garbage."

Suzanne continued, "The things I'm teaching you are like tools in a tool belt. You can use as many as you want and pick the ones that work best for you. We're going to add more tools today and there are several ways we can go. I'll list three directions we can take and you tell me which sounds most interesting to you. We can go deeper into declarations which are an empowerment tool, we can talk about shields which are a protection tool, or we can go deeper into complete conversations which are a release tool. So what do you want to do: empower, protect, or release?"

Crying is actually a good thing. It is a release.

"I like the idea of a shield," I said.

"Great. We'll talk about creating a shield," she said. "Have you seen the movie *Bolt*?"

"No," I said.

"Well, it's a cute animated movie about a hero dog and his adventures," she explained. "One of the characters in the movie is a hamster named Rhino. He is super brave because he runs around in a hamster ball and he knows that nothing can hurt him. He says funny things like 'I eat danger for breakfast!' and 'It can't hurt me, I've got my ball'. What we're going to do is create a shield that you can carry around with you; then wherever you go you can be brave because you're protected."

Okay…," I said hesitantly.

"What would you like your shield to look like? Do you want something like a special outfit that you put on, a shield of light, or something else? It can be anything you imagine," she said.

"Um, right now all I can picture is a hamster ball, but somehow that doesn't make me feel very powerful or protected," I said. "Oh, how about Violet from the movie The Incredibles? She makes a shield that is like a force field bubble that surrounds her."

"Great," Suzanne said, "I want you to visualize creating a force field bubble starting at your feet and growing until it surrounds you, but I want you to leave a hole at the top. Light pours into the hole to fill the bubble and completely surrounds you. What color is the light?" she asked.

"Um, yellow, I guess," I said.

"Okay," she said, "what does it feel like inside your bubble?"

"It's comfortable and safe. It's feels warm," I said.

"Anything else?" she asked.

"I can't think of anything else; if I do can I add it later?" I asked.

"Sure," she said. "Now this bubble will reflect away any negative thoughts and comments from other people, but it will allow in anything positive. Got it?"

"Okay," I said.

"Now we're going to add guards outside your bubble for another layer of protection. What do you want your guards to look like? Do they have shields and armor?" she asked.

"How about angels?" I replied.

"Perfect, how many?" she inquired.

"Twelve," I said.

"Great, where are they standing? Are they in front?" she asked.

"No, they're all around me, like the positions of the numbers on a clock," I responded.

"Excellent, you can move them around if you need to. If you feel that attacks come more from the front or the back, you can ask them to rearrange their positions," she said. "Part of your assignment for next time is every morning you are going to visualize putting on this shield. You now have angels and love shielding and protecting you. They allow good to come in, but anything negative is deflected by the angels and the shield. Got it?"

"Sure," I said, writing it down in my notes.

"Okay, did I already teach you that the fruit doesn't look like the root?" she asked.

"No," I replied.

She drew a simple picture of a tree complete with the roots under the ground, then she drew fruit on the tree.

"The part you see is the fruit. Right now the fruit that you're seeing is that you can't trust anybody and you're comparing and feeling less than everybody around you, but the fruit is not causing the problem; there is something feeding that fruit. In a tree, fruit is fed through the branches, which connect to the trunk, which connects to the main roots, which connect to the feeder roots.

The feeder roots are where the problem begins," she explained. "Those little roots are searching for proof to feed the tiny fruit. The problem is not that everybody is untrustworthy and you're not as good as everybody else, because those things are thoughts that aren't true, but they're a result of whatever is feeding those roots. That's what we want to identify and feed them something different so that we can grow different fruit."

"I think I understand," I said. "We're trying to get to the root of the problem."

"There are three different categories of thinking," she

continued. "The first is 'what I think about me', the second is 'what I think about other people', and the third is 'what I think others think about me'. We're going to work more on declarations. So far your declarations have been in the category 'what I think about me' which is a good start, but we need to address all three categories of thinking. We need to include others in your declarations, something like 'other people value what I have to say.'"

"Oh," I said. "I can see how that would be important."

"Do you have your declarations taped to your bathroom mirror where you can see them every day?" she asked.

"No," I replied, "but I put them on the back of my phone." My phone had a clear cover and I slipped them between the phone and the cover.

"Oh, that's a good idea, but I want you to put them up on the mirror, too. It's good for other people to see your goals and what you're working on," she said. "That way they can help you. Is your family being supportive? What do they think about your singing and what you're working on?"

"They don't know what I'm working on. I tried sharing once and it didn't turn out so well. I actually wait until everybody's gone and hide in the bathroom with the door closed to sing my song. I'm scared to have anybody hear me," I confessed.

Just keep going. Things will change. People will treat you differently as you change.

"Oh," she said, "I'm sorry. Just keep going. Things will change. People will treat you differently as you change."

"Okay, we need to come up with some additional things you can say for your declarations," she said, "Things that include what others think about you. How about, 'I matter and make a difference for good.'"

"I like that," I said, writing it down in my notes.

"How about, 'I am amazing and do great things'?"

I froze. She mistook my silence and said, "You don't like

that one? That's okay, we can choose something else."

"It's not that I don't like it. It's just that I could never say that," I said. "It's not true."

"Okay," she said, "We're going to change directions for a little while. We need to talk about the subconscious some more."

She drew the now familiar picture of a circle divided by a horizontal line and wrote conscious on the top half and subconscious on the bottom half.

"You remember this picture of the way our minds work?" she said. "Things that enter our minds go through the conscious and bounce off this line that separates the conscious from the subconscious."

She drew a line entering the conscious and bouncing off the line to exit again.

"The line that selects what is accepted and what is rejected is called the Reticular Activating System or abbreviated as RAS," Suzanne explained. "The RAS filters the incoming information and affects what you allow into your brain. This system is designed to keep us from getting overloaded with information and also protects us by keeping out information that the mind sees as dangerous and unsafe. When you hear the words 'I am amazing and do great things' your RAS is rejecting that as a dangerous lie, but the truth is that your RAS can't really tell the difference between truth and lies. Your RAS needs to be reprogramed and in order to reprogram it, we need to be able to get past that barrier to give new information to your brain. Once your brain has new information to work with, it can reprogram what the RAS rejects as dangerous lies."

It's not that I don't like it. It's just that I could never say that. It's not true.

"Music is a powerful tool to get past that barrier," she continued. "That's why you've been singing. Music can also help your mind accept your declarations faster. Adding background music allows the declarations to get past the RAS and allows it to enter the brain. What I want you to do is find some music that you can use as background music to play while you say your declarations. It should be powerful, inspiring music that doesn't have words. A soundtrack of epic music is an excellent choice. When you look into the mirror and see yourself saying your declarations with powerful background music, it helps create new pathways in the brain. You can change up the the music depending on what power you need. For example a happy song inspires happiness and a soothing song inspires calmness and a powerful song inspires power. Shake it up and use different things. Variety also helps you get past that RAS."

I tried to sort through the tumble of thoughts that were running through my mind.

Oh, so that's what Erika was talking about when she said that she did declarations with music, was followed immediately by, *This is crazy. I'm not only supposed to imagine up a magic invisible shield to protect me, now I'm going to stand in front of a mirror and speak delusional things to myself with epic music playing in the background? These are actions that I associated with social misfits who try to escape reality by playing Dungeons and Dragons and going Larping.*

"I don't know if I can do this. If anybody found out… my husband would be calling for a straightjacket. What did I get myself into?

Then I remembered something else. It happened at the retreat. It wasn't part of any of the lessons; it actually happened when everybody was packing up to go home. Suzanne checked her phone messages and found a message from her daughter Jessica, a beautiful young woman recently married to a handsome young athlete who had been recruited by a renowned university on a track scholarship.

"Hi Mom, this is Jessica," the message began. "I know you're busy with the women's retreat, but I'm at Max's track meet and he just broke his personal record in the 500 meter hurdles race. This is something he's been working on for five years and hasn't been able to beat it, but today he did and we both know it's because of the declarations and the things that you've been teaching us and we wanted to let you know and to thank you. Talk to you later, bye."

This stuff really works, or at least they really believe it does and they're getting results somehow.

When Suzanne got the message she played it again on speakerphone for us to hear. I remember at the time thinking, *Wow. That's pretty amazing. This stuff really works, or at least they really believe it does and they're getting results somehow. That's awesome.*

This sounds so weird, but I'm going to try it, I thought, *But I'll definitely be hiding in the bathroom with the door closed and the fan turned on.*

I sighed and brought my attention back to what Suzanne was saying. She was talking about creating different pathways.

"Your mind has different pathways like roads," she explained. "You have pathways that are well traveled, and they're like highways. They're fast and easy to travel on. When you try to create a new pathway, a new way of thinking, it's like starting a new dirt trail. Your mind is going to want to go on the fast highway rather than the new slow dirt trail, but if you keep traveling along the dirt trail it will eventually become a dirt road, then a paved road, and it too can become a fast highway. However, it's going to take time and a lot of practice."

We completed the mentoring session and it was time to clear out a few things with the Body Code. Things were going pretty smoothly until she hit on a trapped feeling of 'taken for granted' at around age 27. She needed to know more information before it would clear and I couldn't think of any major event from that time.

"I went to an acupuncturist who also practices Body Code and he found something from that age as well, but I couldn't figure out what it was," I said.

When things don't come immediately to mind, Body Code is a little like playing twenty questions with yes or no answers until you find the right thing. When Suzanne finally found it she let out a little laugh, "It's the thought 'I'm just a mom,'" she said. "I've had that one, too."

"Is that what I was so angry about?" I wondered aloud. "I had my first yelling, swearing complete conversation, but I didn't even know what I was angry about, I was just so mad. Let's see, what was happening when I was about twenty-seven?"

I pondered. My husband had been hired as an airline pilot and was gone for days at a time, leaving me to take care of the house and the yard and the kids all by myself. "Perhaps it's a feeling that I do all the work and he gets all the glory?"

"That could be," she said. "And remember that when the Body Code identifies an age it doesn't mean that's the only time you felt that way; it's just a starting point for discovering those trapped and hidden emotions. *Work on that one. It will take some time.* You're going to need to do some journaling on this one. Write down 'I feel like I'm not of value, that I'm just a mom because...' and write everything you can think of. What does it mean to be 'just a mom.' Get it all out. Remember the picture we drew of the tree, fruit and roots? The fruit is 'I'm just a mom,' but we journal to get to the roots. It may take pages and pages. Dig deep. Then shred it, burn it, or crumple it up and stomp on it, but get rid of it. Those thoughts are garbage."

"Let's see if there are any others that we can identify today," she said.

The feeling of 'worthless' came up again. Shocker. And then the feeling of 'pride'—not the good kind of self worth pride, but the 'I'm better than' negative kind of pride.

"How can I be feeling both worthless and prideful? Aren't they opposites?" I asked.

"Actually they go together frequently," Suzanne said. "We feel worthless, but we are programmed for survival and our survival instincts kick in to fight those feelings. It ends up being a battle of vacillating between feeling worthless and prideful and continues in an unhealthy cycle. We want to develop the healthy kind of pride that is a sense of confidence and self worth. We don't want to look side to side by comparing ourselves with others to create our identity and self worth. That's like wallowing in the mud. We want to look up. You're a child of God. You're amazing, but then you see the people around you and realize that they are also children of God and they're amazing, too. As you lift yourself, you also lift those around you."

"Let's talk a little more about comparing," she continued. "You said that you were struggling with that."

"That's for certain," I admitted.

"How do you feel when you see other people's talents?" she asked.

"To be honest, I try to be happy for them," I said, "but inside I feel like their success emphasizes my weakness and failure."

"Okay," she said, "You played basketball when you were younger, right?"

"Yes," I said.

"Imagine that you're playing basketball," she said, "and the teams are set up so that it's you on one team and the rest of the world on the other team. Do you think you could ever win that game?"

"Obviously not," I replied.

"Right, because if anybody other than you makes a basket then they're winning and you're losing," she said. "Now let's rearrange the teams. If you have other members on your team would you be happy if one of your team members made a basket?"

"Yes," I replied.

"You know that if a team member makes a basket, then it helps you win," she said. "When you're struggling with comparing yourself with those around you, perhaps you could have a complete conversation with them and as a part of that conversation, ask them to join with you and be on your team. If you're on the same team, then you realize that when any member of the team succeeds, it benefits the whole team. If it's you against the whole world, you are going to lose every time."

"That's an interesting perspective" I said. "I like the idea of inviting people to be on my team. I'll give that a try."

A TASTE OF SUCCESS

The following morning I printed out my new declarations (I am loved; I know who I am; I love myself; My words have value; I have the courage to speak my truth; My efforts are noticed and appreciated by other people; I am making a difference for good in the world; and I rejoice in other people's successes) and taped them to my bathroom mirror. I also visualized putting on my shield and played epic music while saying my new list of declarations. I did feel a little silly, but I got through it. I also had a few complete conversations and began inviting other people to be on my team.

I was not sure if those actions were what made the difference or not, but that very day I survived getting a rejection letter for something that I had dared reach outside my comfort zone to try. It was disappointing, but not devastating. I was able to host a dinner that night to welcome a new family that had moved into the neighborhood and be a gracious host.

The following day I was invited to lunch by another friend and former co-worker. I had gone back to work after all my children were in school, but it wasn't as fulfilling as I thought it would be and it created unexpected issues at home. My rigid schedule did not mesh with my husband's constantly changing schedule and we weren't able to see each other for days at a time. If we were in the position of trying to get started out in life, it would be worth the sacrifice, but in our current state, it was causing more harm than good for our family. At the completion of my year contract, I decided not to commit to another term, but I volunteered to help complete a project that I cared about deeply from home where I had more flexibility in my schedule. I had just finished my portion of the project and sent it in. This lunch was a celebration and a thank you for the volunteer service that I had rendered.

I was happy to spend time with my friend, but because of

our previous association, I was afraid that she might ask questions that pertained to my latest personal earthquake aftershock. I almost made it through the lunch without her broaching the subject, but as we were boxing our leftover food to take home, she asked a direct question. I set down my box and answered honestly and directly, while omitting details that might damage another person's reputation. More questions followed and I answered those, as well. She was supportive and it really did feel like we were on the same team. It was rather liberating. A few weeks ago I don't know what I would have done if something like this came up. I would probably have made up an excuse and avoided the lunch altogether and maybe even ended the friendship if I felt that it was too dangerous. I not only survived the lunch, it was actually a healing thing and now I had another member on my 'team'.

Another day we were taking a walk and saw some kids trying to repair the chain on their tandem bicycle. My husband immediately stopped and began to help them. As I watched him, I thought about how much I appreciated his kindness and his skills. I thought about how much richer my life has been because of his influence. I had been seeing him in a different light. I think I was falling in love with my husband. It's not that I ever stopped loving him, it's just that I was starting to remember what attracted me to him in the first place. For a long time I had been terrified of him. Not that he's ever been abusive; I just feared what he thought of me. I guess that meant that I valued his opinion more than anyone else's.

I wanted to try serving again, but wasn't sure if there was a place where my help was needed. I learned about a website called "Justserve.org" that lists service opportunities available by zip code. I entered my zip code and found over a hundred service opportunities within five miles of my house. I found two that I could do right away. One was a need for hygiene kits for incoming refugees. I went to the store with their recommended list of needed items and began gathering supplies. I invited a group of teenagers to help me assemble the supplies into individual kits and put them in gallon-size ziplock bags. Then I delivered the assembled kits to the drop off location with a touch of apprehension. My last attempts at service didn't turn out so well. I was nervous that I was going to the wrong location or I misread the instructions or did something else wrong, but when I arrived and delivered the kits it was the right place and they were very appreciative. I gave a sigh of relief. *That wasn't so bad*, I thought. *I can do this.*

The next service opportunity was to help at a local food bank. When I told my family that I wanted to go, they surprised me by offering to go with me. I called to make an appointment and we arrived at a tiny hidden building that I never knew existed until that day. The food bank receives donations, but sometimes the food is spoiled. Our first assignment was to go through boxes of bread to sort out the good bread from the moldy bread. We sorted through an entire wall of moving sized boxes full of bread. When that was finished we helped organize donated food onto shelves so workers could easily see what was available to give to those in need. The work wasn't difficult, but it felt good. I learned that donation levels taper off during the summer time and there wasn't as much food to go around. People go on vacations and forget that there are hungry people in their neighborhoods. During the holidays the shelves of the food banks fill as people remember to reach out to others. I had never even considered that fluctuation. I guess I fit in the same category as everybody else. I made a mental note to donate year round rather than only during the winter season.

That wasn't so bad, I thought. I can do this.

Our house has an outbuilding that serves as my husband's workshop. He is always building something. Sometimes the projects turn out awesome and sometimes they don't work out so well, but he is driven by a need to create. The current shop project is a hovercraft. One day, during the same week that we went to the food bank, I went into the shop to see how his project was progressing. Usually I just take a look and then return to the house, but this day I stayed a while and listened while he talked about what he'd done and what needed to be done next. I watched while he applied strips of fiberglass cloth to cover the seams and I held the roll of fiberglass for him while he cut it to the proper length. Then I stayed to watch as he applied the resin to the fiberglass strips with a paintbrush.

I realized that it had been a long time since I did that.

After a while I turned to leave and he said, "Thanks for coming out to watch and help today. I really appreciate it."

I realized that it had been a long time since I did that.

Another night that week we camped out in our tent trailer. The tent trailer was pretty new to us; I had only slept in it one other time and that was in the late autumn when we bought it. It was a horrible, uncomfortable, freezing, miserable, sleepless night, and I was reluctant to try again. Lewis had really tried to ensure that the next time would be a better experience. He bought me a new, warmer sleeping bag for Christmas and a mattress topper and kept asking me to go again. I was not remotely interested in trying a winter camping trip; I didn't care how warm the sleeping bag was supposed to be. As far as I was concerned, the tent trailer could find a new home elsewhere. However, now it was the beginning of summer, and so I agreed to give it another try. I snuggled in my new sleeping bag and was relieved that I didn't feel every knot and every screw in every board through the new mattress topper. It was a pleasant night and I appreciated the effort that he had made to make it more comfortable for me.

We wanted to canoe down the Jordan River again. One

of my daughters had been away to college when we went the first time, so the plan was for me to go with my two daughters. Lewis loaded the canoes; we have one two person canoe and another single person canoe. He had built the light, fabric covered single place canoe last year in his shop. He helped us put them in the water and drove to the take out point to pick us up. When we arrived at the takeout point, he was there waiting for us and helped us take out the canoes and load them back on the truck. He even picked up lunch at Apollo Burger so we could have a picnic in the park. *My husband is awesome*, I thought. *I'm so fortunate to have him in my life.*

THE SECOND MONTH

It had been a month since I began this journey. I still had a long way to go, but life was already so much brighter. I was in a very different place than I was when I received the invitation to attend a women's retreat. I wasn't sure if my actions had changed or not, but I felt different inside.

It was now time for another Body Code session with Suzanne.

"I'm proud of you for being so consistent in returning and reporting your progress in your personal tracking forms," Suzanne began. "You haven't missed a day. I can tell that you really want to progress. That's the way I was. I just ate it up. I spent at least an hour a day working on myself."

"I'm probably spending that much time each day as well," I replied. "I want to keep moving forward and I have such a long way to go."

"Good job," she said. "The more you do every day, the faster you will progress. Okay, let's get started. Is there anything in particular that you want to work on today?"

"No," I replied. "Just follow the direction that my body says I need the most."

"All right," she said. "Let's see. It looks like the priority is a mental image that you have of yourself. That's great. I love images because we can work to create a new image in our next mentoring session. That's one of the reasons that I love working with the Body Code and mentoring together. The Body Code can identify things that need to be removed and then the mentoring tools can help to repair and rebuild."

"Okay," she continued. "This is the image that you have of yourself. The first descriptive word is humiliation. That's an unusual word. Does that sound right?"

"Yes," I replied.

"Why would you feel humiliated?" she inquired.

"Because I'm not good enough," I began. "I'm ashamed of my insignificance. I'm ashamed of my very being. I always want to disappear and hide."

"I would never have guessed that," she said. "You seem so put together all the time. No wonder you have felt like a fraud. Well, we're going to change that," she said. "Now the next word is unworthy and the next is worthless. Does that sound right?"

"Yes," I replied. "That pretty much describes me: humiliated, unworthy, and worthless."

"This mental image is like a blueprint in your mind," she explained. "Humiliation, unworthiness, and worthlessness have been the blueprint for your identity. Your mind will refer to this blueprint for all your thoughts and all your actions so it can build everything according to the plans. You need to do what you can to release this old blueprint and create a new one."

"You can do journaling to address these feelings," she continued. "You can start by writing, 'I feel humiliated because…', and things like that."

"Let's work on the next trapped emotion," she said. "This one is from age six again; it's depression but we need to know more. Why would you be feeling depressed?"

"Because I'm unimportant," I said. "I am invisible."

"Invisible?" she said. "I've heard you use that word a lot. We'll need to address that, too. Are you doing any releases? Have you been doing journaling?"

"No," I replied, "That wasn't on the list of assignments. I've been doing declarations and singing, though."

"All right," she said, "you need to add journaling. You're doing things to add positive, but you also need to release the negative. Do you remember the ping pong ball demonstration?"

"Yes," I replied.

"Good," she said. "Those negative feelings are in there and they'll stay in there until you take them out. Do you understand journaling? I've talked about it and I've assumed that you knew what to do."

"I kind of understand," I said, "It's writing down things that come to mind and then destroying it."

"Okay," she said, "Let me explain that a little better. Journaling can also be called taking out the trash. Do you remember the image of the fruit tree and the roots?"

"Yes," I said.

"All right," Suzanne continued. "Journaling is a way to get to the root of the problem. When I was only doing Body Code and I was working on myself, I kept coming up with 'worthless' and I would remove it but it kept coming back. I was removing the fruit, but it kept growing back. I hadn't addressed the root of the problem because I didn't know what the root was. Complete conversations are a verbal release and they give you a chance to say what you were never able to say. Journaling gets deeper. It helps you understand yourself better and get to the root of the problem."

> *I was removing the fruit, but it kept growing back.*

"Think about that image of the fruit tree," she instructed. "When you're journaling you are starting with the fruit which is the part that you see. You might write, 'I feel invisible because...' across the top of the page. Then put the pen on the paper and write anything and everything that comes into your mind. Even if it seems strange, write it. What you're writing is like the branch that supports the fruit."

"When you can't think of anything else to write you stop. Thank your body for what it found. Say, 'That was awesome. Thanks for finding that, now take me deeper,' put the pen down on the next line and start writing again. Write anything and everything that comes to mind. This will be like the trunk that holds the branch that supports the fruit. When you can't think of anything else to write, stop again. Thank you body for what it found and ask it to take you deeper. It may take pages and pages of writing to finally get to the root of the problem. As you write, you will find some golden nuggets. These will be truths that you'll want to remember. Copy those things onto a separate place before you destroy the paper. This process will take a long time at first, but after practicing, you'll be able to get to the root much quicker. When I started my journey to healing, I wrote for an hour every day. I wrote and wrote and wrote."

"Does it have to be handwritten?" I asked. "When we were at the retreat and I was taking all those notes, my arm was so sore by the end of the day. I'm not used to doing a lot of handwriting. Can I just type on the computer?"

"Well," she said. "It's so much better if you can hand write it because that makes a physical connection between your body and the pen and the paper to extract all those thoughts and feelings onto the page. One thing you can do to make it easier is don't worry about writing legibly. Just relax and let your hand flow. It doesn't matter if you can't read it afterwards because you're just going to destroy it anyway."

"It's interesting that your arm hurts," she went on. "We can work on that with the Body Code in another session. Trapped feelings can settle in different parts of the body and affect us physically. You're a writer; it makes sense that some emotions got trapped in your arm. We'll see if we can get them out; hopefully that will help."

GOOD ENOUGH?

Another day had passed and I still hadn't done any journaling. I know now that I was avoiding it, but I wasn't sure why. I had tried to be strictly obedient with everything that Suzanne has asked me to do, except for this one thing. The list of topics that I was supposed to be journaling kept getting longer and longer, but I didn't even want to start it.

I didn't like writing freehand. My handwriting is terrible. I've never had neat girly handwriting with cute curlicues. I blame it on being left handed, but it's probably not really that. Also my hand, wrist, tendons, and arm muscles protested when I tried to write. It was terribly uncomfortable.

I liked the complete conversation tool. I had some success with that, but I often couldn't think of anything to say. Nothing came to mind. I hadn't had any success with journaling yet. We made a few attempts at the retreat, but I didn't have time to finish anything. The only one I remember at all is the letter we were supposed to write to our body, and I didn't finish that one or destroy it.

Perhaps I was scared to dig deeper. I didn't want any more ping pong balls to surface. I didn't want to deal with painful issues. Why couldn't they just go away on their own? Why did I need to acknowledge them first and remember them at all? It felt like going backwards and I wanted to move forwards.

I was in a pretty good place. Wasn't it good enough? Yesterday my son, a college student, asked for advice with a homework assignment for his communications class. He was supposed to identify an unhealthy relationship and take steps to correct it. He had a discussion with his dad and sister and they couldn't think of any unhealthy relationships in our home; they recommended that he think about his relationships with his friends as a source for his assignment. That one raised my eyebrows a bit. That indicated that my family seems to be satisfied with my progress and everybody was happy with the way things were.

I wasn't feeling depressed anymore, and although I still struggled with anxiety somewhat, I could function and even contribute. It was good, and yet it was recently brought to my attention that my mental image of myself consisted of humiliation, unworthiness, worthlessness, and invisibility. That was the blueprint for my identity. That was obviously not good. I was going to have to come face to face with the root of my identity in order to move forward and I really, really didn't want to. I wanted to bury it so deeply that I never had to think about it again. Was there no other way?

I think I'll go for a bike ride rather than deal with it right now.

PING PONG BALLS

"Are you okay?" my daughter asked.

"I'm fine," I said dismissively and changed the subject.

The truth is that I was not fine. I felt disturbed and angry. I tried one of those stupid journaling things and now my mind was a whirl. I started with "I feel worthless because…" but the lines seemed to blur between all the sections of my messed up blueprint of identity. Five pages later I tore it up and the paper was gone, but it was not out of my head yet.

Some of the things that came up were really bothering me. They were experiences at school that I had long forgotten. I felt rather invisible at home, so I threw myself into my schoolwork. I was a good student and got excellent grades. In high school I was ranked number one out of the seven hundred graduating seniors. I had two friends who were a very close second and third and it was a challenge to maintain that top spot. The three of us were both friends and adversaries.

When we took the ACT test, I got a very good score, high enough to get a four year scholarship at the university of my choice. My score also had the prideful benefit of beating my two friends. When an opportunity came to retake the ACT I didn't bother because I didn't need to, but my friends retook the test and improved their scores. One beat me by one point and the other beat me by two points. I didn't care; I didn't think it mattered. However, *I didn't care; I didn't think it mattered.* when the school determined the valedictorian, they chose to use the ACT as the deciding factor rather than GPA. My friend who beat me by two points was selected as valedictorian, the friend who had beaten my by one point was selected as salutatorian, and I was given nothing. It felt like they literally changed the rules just to exclude me. I was devastated and humiliated. This was one time in my life when my mother went to bat for me and visited the school to ask why they had done this. Their response was to invite me to be "co-salutatorian" which is a term they made up to mean "third place."

I was invited to the end-of-the-year award assembly. My friend who had been awarded the honor of valedictorian was called up to the stage again and again to receive award after award, but they didn't even call my name for honor roll. It was as if they had invited me for the sole purpose of rubbing my defeat in my face. Afterwards an administrator handed me a couple pieces of paper and said, "They forgot to call out your name. Here are your certificates." There was no apology and no announcement of correction. I was once again humiliated and passed over.

Top students were selected in various categories and were honored with a picture and plaque hanging in the main hall. I was selected as top overall scholar. However, when I returned to the school the following year to support a friend's

I was once again humiliated and passed over.

music concert, I noticed that all the pictures of the top scholars from the previous year were still hanging in the hallway except mine. I had been taken down and symbolically erased. I was no longer attending the school, but they still found ways to belittle and humiliate me.

This happened decades ago. Not a soul on earth cares that I didn't get to be valedictorian, or didn't have my name called at an awards assembly or had my picture removed from the wall. I had completely forgotten about it until then, and it felt like it happened yesterday. The shame, humiliation, and anger were as fresh as wet paint. My academic success had been my source of identity and pride, the one thing I knew I was good at, and they flushed it and me down the toilet.

I think I'm going to have a little chat with the faculty and administration of the High School that served during the year when I graduated. I think it's time for my second yelling, swearing complete conversation.

THE FIRST SHARE

The complete conversation did not go the way I expected. I thought I would be yelling, but instead I was sobbing. This is also the very first time that when it came to the part where I'm supposed to say sorry and apologize that I couldn't think of anything that I'd done wrong. I racked my brain and couldn't come up with a single thing that was my fault, so I simply said, "I'm sorry for feeling that way, please forgive me." Then completed the series with a conversation with God and another with my seventeen year-old self. The experience was strangely cathartic. The recently dug up memory was still fresh in my mind, but the associated feelings of shame and anger dissipated. It simply didn't matter as much anymore. I was glad that there were two tools for releasing negative emotions. The journaling brought it up, but didn't get rid of it. Maybe I was not doing it right. I don't know. I was still learning, but it took the complete conversation to be able to let it go.

I felt safe enough and strong enough after the complete conversation to do something I hadn't dared do before. I shared this journal with my adult children and allowed them to read it. It was so scary to invite them into the secret recesses of my soul which leaves me vulnerable, but each one responded with love and support. Many tears were shed as they became aware of my struggles, heartache, and pain. I had more members on my team. I wasn't so alone. Someday I would be brave enough to share this with my husband, but I feared being vulnerable to him more than anyone.

ANOTHER LONG-FORGOTTEN MEMORY

Yet another ping pong ball surfaced. It amazes me the things that can be erased from our thoughts. A friend mentioned being sexually molested as a child, and it triggered another long-forgotten memory. I was about eight years old. It wasn't a family member, which was wonderful because I haven't seen this person in years and will probably never see him again. I now see that his primary objective was to dominate and humiliate me. The clear message was, "I am more powerful than you and can do anything to you that I want."

I don't remember a lot of detail except him laughing at me. I never told anyone because I was humiliated and ashamed. It's so unfair that a perpetrator transfers the guilt and shame to the victim.

I chose to let this one go. He shamed me long enough.

WHAT IT MEANS TO BE A WOMAN

I needed a few days to recover before I was ready to journal again and tackle the next ping pong ball of pain. I got a triple whammy. Apparently I have issues with my roles as a woman, mother, and wife.

My thoughts on being a woman:

First of all, I hated the biological fact that men are stronger than women. It made me so angry. I'll never forget the day that I realized that my oldest son had surpassed me in strength. We were helping a neighbor install sod in their backyard. I struggled to lift the heavy rolls of sod and set them in place. Then I noticed that my teenage son could lift them with ease. This was my little boy who I brought into the world as a helpless baby. I carried him around and nurtured him and took care of him and now he was taller and stronger than I was. Although I was proud of him for using his strength in service, I was also jealous that what was so difficult for me was easy for him. We were doing the exact same job, but it was harder for me than for him. Furthermore, my husband was strong enough to outwork us both with the same amount of effort. It was so unfair.

Soon after this experience I had a second blow to my ego. We were carrying a large glass sliding door to install in an addition we were making to the house. I struggled as I carried my end of the heavy door. My son and his friend came over to help. I greatly appreciated the help, but I did not appreciate the way my son's friend brushed me aside like I was an insect.

"Move out of the way. We got this," he said dismissively.

I was shocked and angry at this snot-nosed kid who treated me like I was helpless. My husband and I built our house together. Not the kind of 'built a house' where you choose the tile and paint colors and give instructions to the contractor; but the kind of 'built a house' where you cut rebar, pour cement, pound nails, install shingles, sand drywall, lay tile and paint walls. I had done it all. I was not weak and helpless because I am a female, and yet as I stepped aside to allow the boys to move the heavy door, they lifted it with ease. The evidence was before me that they were indeed stronger than I was and it made me mad. It was so unfair.

Who was responsible for this unequal distribution of physical power? Did I blame evolution or God? Either way it totally sucked. Men are physically more powerful, which gives an obvious advantage in a 'might makes right' world. Whenever I read a book like *Memoirs of a Geisha*, *The Good Earth*, or *A Thousand Splendid Suns* which are set in misogynistic cultures, I got angry. How could anyone think of women as second class citizens, servants, or chattel?

Are men and women the same? Are they different?

The roles of men and women have been a recurring conundrum throughout global history. Are men and women the same? Are they different? And if they're different then which gender is superior?

I'm grateful that I live in a time and a place where women are valued, but even here in the United States we don't have it sorted out. In the 1950s Marilyn Monroe was the iconic symbol of the ideal woman. Her roles in the movies *How to Marry a Millionaire* and *Gentlemen Prefer Blondes* exemplify the expectation of women. In these movies the differences between men and women are emphasized and exaggerated. Women use their feminine charm to lure and manipulate men, but they have little to offer besides their beauty.

Nowadays the expected role of women is a polar opposite from that of the 1950's. Whereas being a woman once meant being soft, curvy, but helplessly dependent, now the ideal woman is a powerful and sexy comic book superhero. She must be all powerful and be able to do everything without any assistance whatsoever.

The differences between men and women are minimized and repudiated. Femininity and a proclivity towards nurturing are eschewed as weakness. Furthermore, even if she accomplishes the new ideal, she is still replaceable. Think of all the James Bond movies; he finds a woman who meets every criteria, but in the next movie she is never mentioned again, and he simply finds another one.

I would prefer to be Black Widow or Wonder Woman than the characters portrayed by Marilyn Monroe, but what if I didn't agree with either of the expectation options listed above? I didn't want to sit still and look pretty, nor did I want to be expected to carry the whole world on my shoulders. Wasn't there something in between? What if I wanted to be feminine and nurturing and strong and capable and useful and valued?

Yes, I struggled with the definition of what it means to be a woman, but I was not the only one who has grappled with this gender identity crisis. People wonder if gender matters at all. We can't seem to be able to figure out a way to respect and value differences without comparing and competing.

It brought to mind the lesson we had at the women's retreat on complementary colors. Perhaps men and women are complementary; not that they need to be the same, or that one is better than the other, but that they are different so that they can complete each other as equal partners.

I decided to have a group complete conversation with all the men in the world as part of the process of coming to terms with a definition of womanhood that I could accept. I even tried inviting them to be on my team so I wouldn't feel like I'm competing against them in an ever losing battle. I wasn't sure that it would solve anything, but it was worth a try

I AM MY KIDS' MOM

My thoughts on being a mom:

I love it when Dr. Laura Schlessinger introduces herself by saying, "I am my kids' mom." Her words add validation to the important role of motherhood. However, people do not read her books or listen to her radio program because she is a mom; they value and respect her because of her education and professional expertise. It is very difficult for a woman who is "just a mom" to be valued in our society.

When I was a school teacher, although it's not a very lucrative career, people honored and respected the altruistic sacrifices made for the benefit of the rising generation. However, in order for those sacrifices to count, apparently they must be made for other people's children. If you make those same sacrifices for your own children then you're not valued as a productive member of society.

I had the experience of being a stay at home mom and it was very, very difficult. I also had the experience of being a working mom and it was harder. It was not harder because going to work was more difficult than taking care of children at home; it was harder because in addition to all the stresses and challenges at work, a mom is still a mom, with all the mom responsibilities. There was just less time and energy to accomplish them. I also had a lot of guilt. When illness, accidents and emergencies happened, I wasn't able to take care of things in the manner that I wanted. Working simply did not allow for the flexibility and adaptability necessary for the role of mothering. We made a decision that having me home with our children was more important than money.

If I were a single mom, I'd have no choice but to do it all on my own, but since I have a companion, we can divide the labor.

One thing that we could not divide equally was who has the babies. I couldn't say, "Okay, I had the last one so it's your turn to have the next one." Nature decided that one for us. Having the babies would be my job. So we decided to divide the labor in the traditional way. He would provide the necessities of life and I would be primarily responsible for the nurturing of our children, but we would help each other as equal partners.

Just because we made a conscious and informed decision, it still didn't make it easy. When I quit my job to be a stay at home mom years ago when my first child was born, I was the primary provider for our family. My income was nearly twice that of my husband's income since he was still in training for his chosen profession. Quitting my job meant certain deprivation. It would mean careful budgeting and doing without a lot of things. I was also keenly aware that this decision would leave me vulnerable since I had to rely on another person for my support, and it terrified me. My choice to be a stay at home mom wasn't a sign of weakness; it took a tremendous amount of courage and required a giant leap of faith.

I was also keenly aware that this decision would leave me vulnerable ...

I was still in the process of getting used to these new adjustments of being a stay at home mom when a former high school classmate called out of the blue. I hadn't heard from her in years. Apparently she had felt in competition with me in high school, but to be candidly honest, I had never even noticed. I had only recognized two people as my academic peers and rivals and this girl had never even been in the running. She was calling for the sole purpose to boast about her successes and let me know how truly exceptional she really was. I listened with baffled curiosity as she listed all of her accomplishments, but didn't panic until she asked what I was doing now.

"Well, actually, I'm a mom and I'm home taking care of my

family," I admitted with hesitation.

"I could never do that," she exclaimed with horror, "I would go brain dead. You're wasting your life and you were supposed to be so smart." She gloated in her ultimate triumph over me.

For the three days following her phone call, I walked around in a daze. Was I wasting my life? Had I made the wrong decision? Within a month I received another phone call from a former classmate I hadn't heard from in years. Although he was not nearly as brash as the first caller had been, he also listed his successes and many accolades and then laughed when he learned that I was "just a mom." I felt humiliated.

I chose to be a mother. I love my children and wouldn't have it any other way, and yet I hate being weighed, measured, and found wanting. I hate that people judge me and assume that I'm a stay at home mom because I am unqualified to do anything else.

I chose to be a mother. I love my children and wouldn't have it any other way ...

The judgement is pretty universal, but the condemnation is usually felt most vehemently from other women. In some conversations, although I've said nothing inflamatory, I can feel a woman's defensiveness radiating towards me in the thoughts, "What, you think you're a better mother than I am just because you stay at home?" Other times the thoughts or words are more condescending, "You obviously aren't as capable as I am. I can do everything you do, bring home the bacon, and make a difference in the world."

I saw a funny, yet sadly enlightening youtube video produced by Similac and Publicis Kaplan Thaler called "The Mother 'Hood." In the video, groups of similarly minded mothers are taking verbal jabs at other groups who have a different approach. The breastfeeding mothers judge and condemn the bottle feeding moms, the stay at home moms take jabs at the working moms and everybody is judging and condemning everybody else until they're ready to strike blows. Suddenly they notice a runaway stroller going down a hill and everybody rushes together to save the baby.

The final words of the video are "No matter what our beliefs, we are parents first. Welcome to the sisterhood of motherhood." I really liked that conclusion. Isn't this job hard enough without tearing each other down? Isn't it wonderful that there's more than one right way to do things?

In trying to deal with my issues of my role of being a mother I had a group complete conversation with all the women in the world and invited them to be on my team. I also needed to have a chat with a couple of former high school classmates.

HUSBANDS AND WIVES

My thoughts on being a wife:

I was so jealous of my husband. It was so unfair that he got all the recognition and glory. People think he is so awesome, and he is, but I hate the fact that he's so much cooler than I am. If you take a look at his resume, you'd think, "Wow!" and if you look at mine, you'd think, "Oh." Once, long ago, our accomplishments seemed pretty equivalent, but now he sounds so amazing. He is an airline pilot, he is an author, he builds airplanes and canoes and hovercrafts, etc. and I'm "just a mom." Nothing I had done looked amazing to anybody. I was like the drab little peafowl hen next to her peacock husband. Once again, I was invisible.

Our roles were so unfair. I was the one who had to change my name to take his. I was the one who sacrificed my body to bring children into the world. Anything that was mundane, repetitive, boring, annoying, messy, or uncomfortable was my job. Furthermore, nothing I did ever stayed done. I made dinner; it got eaten. I changed a diaper; it got pooped on. I washed clothes; they got dirty. I cleaned the house; it got messy again. I mowed the lawn; the grass grew. I pulled out the weeds, and they simply grew back.

When our kids were growing up, Lewis would be gone at work for days at a time while I took care of the home, yard and children by myself. When he came home from a trip all the kids would rush to him with hugs and cries of joy. He was a superstar. It was the airport scene of my youth all over again.

I made children do their homework, brush their teeth and clean their rooms, while he bought them ice cream and took them for play dates that he called "looking for trouble." My grown children often reenact a story of one day years ago when I lost it. I can't remember the circumstances that led to it, but I suddenly jumped up and began pantomiming a lion tamer flicking an imaginary whip. I said, "This is the mom. Clean your room!"

I flicked my imaginary whip. "Brush your teeth!"

I flicked my imaginary whip again. "Do your homework!"

Down came the imaginary whip again."Practice the piano!"

I again brought down the imaginary whip. Then I changed from a lion tamer into a fairy and danced around the kitchen saying, "This is the dad, I get to be the fairy godfather. Let's go play. Who wants to go looking for trouble? Let's go get ice cream."

My family was startled at first by my unexpected outburst and then began to laugh. It was funny, but oh so true.

Did I want to heal or did I want to be validated in my anger? As memories resurfaced and feelings clarified, it could go either way. It would be determined by what I chose to do with those memories and feelings. Did I feed my jealousy and anger or let it go?

Did I feed my jealousy and anger or let it go?

Thinking about dealing with anger reminds me of an experience with one of my sons who has an autism spectrum disorder. When he was a little boy and I took him and his younger sister on an outing to the park, she would always emerge with a new friend and he would emerge with a new enemy. My daughter would say something like, "Mom, I met a girl and she was so nice; we played on the slide together and we played tag."

My son would say, "Mom do you see that boy over there? He is such a jerk. Do you know what he did? ..." He was always angry and felt completely self justified that it was entirely the other guy's fault. I didn't know about the phrase "if you spot if you got it," but it certainly applied.

We were meeting regularly with a counselor to help him with some behavioral issues and his anger management issues. In one of the sessions, the counselor was teaching about anger.

"Anger gives a false sense of power and justice," he said, "but it is a counterfeit. It is not real power and it is not real justice." He went on to teach some tools my son could use to help him curb his anger.

It took a long time and a lot of effort, but my son metamorphosed from a whirling dervish of destructive fury to an admirable and remarkable young man. He chose peace and healing and it transformed him. I am proud of my son. He was a good example to me. I wanted to be able to do what he did. I wanted to choose peace and healing.

I needed to have one, or perhaps several, complete conversations with my husband. I also needed to invite him to be on my team. If there's one person in the whole world that I needed to be on my team, it was him. I couldn't be in competition with him. Being jealous of his accomplishments didn't do me any good. The truth was that he shared everything with me. When he succeeded, I won, too. The richest experiences of my life have come because of him. Without him I wouldn't have my children and the wonderful memories that we've made. In turn, the most rewarding experiences of his life came because of me. Our family is his joy as well, and that would never have happened without me. I felt glad that he is awesome. I wouldn't want it any other way. I was glad that he was my companion and partner.

I love him.

THE THIRD MENTORING SESSION

I was looking forward to the next mentoring session. When I filled out the pre-appointment questionnaire I had some positive answers and I expected this one to be uplifting and easy. I figured that I had already gone through the hard stuff. I thought this session would be a breeze.

I was dead wrong. Instead it was disturbing and confusing and I learned that I was way more messed up than I ever thought possible. I hit another wall. I learned some new things about myself that I didn't like and I didn't want to face them. This was so hard and felt so dangerous and unsafe. I just wanted to give up and make the pain, shame, and discomfort stop.

"I was so excited to see your answers on the questionnaire," Suzanne said. "For the one word to describe yourself, you put 'happy'. I'm thrilled that you're having success."

"Thanks," I said.

"On your list of successes since our last visit, it says you accepted a compliment," she said. "What was the compliment?"

"Actually, I don't remember," I confessed, "I was just trying to find ten successes since our last visit and I read through my personal tracking form and it said, 'accepted a compliment' as one of the things. I can't remember what it was, just that I was proud of myself for not rejecting it."

"Well done," she said. "Often when people get a compliment they reflexively brush it away. If you watch people they actually use body language by physically holding up their hand to block it or flick it away. I didn't realize I was doing that until someone called me on it, 'Why did you brush away my compliment?' she asked, and I didn't have an answer. When someone gives you a compliment, draw it into you. Actually bring your hand to your heart and draw it into you."

She made a motion with her arm bringing her hand to her heart to demonstrate.

"Also you don't need to feel obligated to give a compliment in return. It's okay just to say 'thank you' or you can say 'thank you, you're so kind.' You're doing great, I'm so proud of you."

"Thank you," I said.

"Remember to draw it into you and bring your hand to your heart," she admonished.

"Oh," I said. I hadn't realized that was a test. *Sheesh*, I thought. *Instant fail. I'm not just supposed to listen and take notes, I'm actually supposed to do it.*

I tried it and it felt awkward.

"I also noticed on your questionnaire that you survived a rejection," she said, "Tell me about that."

"Well, my daughter Sarah wrote a book and we're self publishing it. The stories and writing style were awesome, but the original version was in desperate need of editing. There were so many errors that we wouldn't even be able to give copies to grandparents," I said. "So I've spent the past several months going through it, making corrections, working with the publishing company and things like that getting it ready to print. Now that it's finished I've been writing letters to stores to ask them to offer it and I got a rejection letter from one because their profit margin wasn't high enough to carry it."

"Why are you doing all this?" she asked. "Why isn't Sarah doing it?"

"She's been super busy with college and work," I explained. "She simply didn't have time."

"So are you going to be okay that you do all this work, but she gets all the credit?" she asked.

"Of course," I replied. "She's my daughter. I'm proud of her and love to see her be successful."

"I see," Suzanne said, "and is your name on the cover, too?"

"No," I said taken aback.

"Did you know that you can share credit on a joint effort?" she said. "You can include 'edited by ...' and have your name included, too."

"That wouldn't be right," I said. "They're her stories."

Actually, Sarah had offered exactly what Suzanne was suggesting.

"Your name should be on the cover too," Sarah had told me one day. "You've put more time and effort into the project than I have."

"Oh no," I refused, "All the stories are yours, the cute and playful writing style is yours. All I did was clean it up so your awesome work could shine through."

Suzanne was still talking, so I had to bring my attention back to the present.

"Did you realize that you consistently put yourself in a sacrificial position?" she asked. "You're always giving, which is good, but you never allow yourself to receive. You're starving yourself."

I didn't like the way this conversation was going. I was getting chewed out for serving and doing good? Isn't that what moms are supposed to do?

You're always giving, which is good, but you never allow yourself to receive. You're starving yourself.

"I'm going to teach you about the principle of 'give and recieve,'" she said. She drew a simple picture of lever balanced on a fulcrum. "Do you remember playing on a teeter-totter when you were little?"

"Yes," I replied.

"What happens on a teeter-totter when one person is a lot heavier than the other person?" she asked.

"Well, one person stays down on one end," I said, "and the

other person stays up on the other end and it doesn't move."

"Right," she said. "And is it fun for either person?"

"No, not really," I said.

"This is like the principle of give and receive," she explained. "When you're giving all the time it's like you're down on the ground lifting the other person up, but you also need to allow them to lift you up. People who do all the work and carry everybody else wear themselves out. Furthermore, it isn't good for the person who is being carried all the time. They want to feel useful and needed, too. The best relationships are give and take with two equal partners giving and receiving like the teeter-totter going back and forth. There needs to be a balance of give and receive in order to have joy."

I didn't really know how to receive. The idea was strange and uncomfortable.

I never considered that. I just thought I was supposed to serve. I didn't really know how to receive. The idea was strange and uncomfortable. I was grateful when she finally changed the subject.

"On your questionnaire you also mentioned that you've talked to your kids. What did they say? How did they respond?" she asked.

"Well, I wrote down what I've been doing to heal and let them read it, and they were very supportive," I said.

"You didn't tell them you wrote it?" she queried.

"Well, yes," I said.

"Okay, so you're sort of finding your voice, but you don't have it all the way yet," she clarified. "You haven't dared have a conversation with them in person yet."

"Oh, is that what that means?" I said disappointed.

"Have you shared with Lewis yet?" she probed.

"No way," I replied. "That's way too scary."

"At some point you're going to need to talk with him,"

she said. "I remember talking with my husband and he was shocked when he realized that I didn't feel emotionally safe with him. It was a real eye opener for him. We both had to make some changes, but it is amazing. Now he keeps saying, 'We make such an awesome team,' and that's what we are. We are a team. Like the teeter-totter example, relationships are better when both people are contributing as equal partners. It's more fun."

"Okay," she continued. "We had planned earlier to work on creating a new mental image for you today, but you're not ready for that yet. When I saw what you wrote on your questionnaire about the obstacles that you're facing and that you don't want to bring up new ping pong balls and that you have a lot of anger and jealousy in you, I realized that you're so full of garbage that there isn't room for a new image yet. We need to work on clearing out the garbage first so there is enough room for something new."

My shoulders sagged with the weight of my failure and shame, not to mention the dread that I would have to face more of my garbage. Why wouldn't it just go away?

VISUALIZATION

"We're going to try something different today," she said. "You're going to do a visualization. This can be a very powerful tool to get rid of garbage."

"Okay," I said.

"I want you to close your eyes and visualize a mountain meadow. Tell me what you see," she instructed.

"There is a meadow with grass and wildflowers," I said.

"Good, what else do you see? What does it feel like?" she asked.

"The sun is shining, but there is also a soft breeze blowing. I see trees on the mountain slopes on either side," I added.

"Good, what kind of trees? What do they look like? How does it feel?" she asked.

"There are evergreens and aspens," I said. "The leaves of the aspens are quaking gently. It feels comfortable and peaceful."

"Okay," she said, "As you're looking across at the trees you see a figure begin to emerge."

In my mind the scene changed at once; the peace was gone and I was instantly on my guard to protect myself from the intruder. I saw an ominous hooded figure emerge from the woods which had turned dark and menacing. I thought this was a test to practice using my shield that I learned about in the last mentoring session. I braced myself for the attack.

"He is dressed all in white," Suzanne said. "You recognize that it is the Savior."

My mind reeled. This was not the direction that I was expecting this to go and I was surprised to realize that I preferred the idea of facing a hooded foe.

"What does He do? What does He say to you?" she asked.

I hesitated. I didn't know how to answer. I tried to change

my mental image from the dark hooded figure to the Savior and waited for my imagination to fill in the next step. In my mind's eye the Savior just stood there and we eyed each other warily. It was like the experience of seeing someone in the grocery store and you know that you know them from somewhere, but you can't remember their name so you hurry to the next aisle and hope they don't see you. It was that kind of awkward. I was pretty sure that wasn't the response Suzanne was hoping for so I tried to think of what the Savior was supposed to do. In the paintings He's always welcoming and hugging people, so I tried to make the Savior image in my visualization reach out to me. He stretched out his arms in a wooden, perfunctory manner.

It was awkward. I was pretty sure that wasn't the response Suzanne was hoping for.

"Um, He's reaching out to me."

It was uttered as more of a question than a statement.

"And what do you do?" she asked.

"Um, I go to Him and embrace," I said. The figures in my visualization hugged briefly and awkwardly then quickly stepped apart.

"Okay," she went on. "The savior has come to take away your burdens. Are you willing to give them to Him?"

"Yes," I said, but in my mind I wasn't sure. The Christ figure in my visualization looked annoyed and impatient. It was a look that I've seen when asking a child to take out the garbage and their eyes say, "Okay, I'll do it if I have to, but I have other things I'd rather be doing."

"All right," she said, "You pull out a burden from your body. What is the burden and what does it look like?"

"It's anger," I said, "It is dark and looks like a tangled ball of string, but it doesn't hold still. It's writhing."

"Can you get it out?" she asked.

"I'm trying to, but as I pull there is still a dangling string and it goes so deep that it doesn't seem to have an end," I said.

"Keep pulling," she said, "Can you reach the end of the string?"

"I think so," I said.

"Where is it coming from? What part of your body?" she asked.

"I think it's coming from my heart," I said, "but I'm not sure. It might be in my head as well."

"What are you angry about?" she pressed.

"I'm angry that men are stronger than women. I'm angry at God for making us that way. I'm angry that it's so unfair," I said.

She kept asking horrible questions that I didn't want to answer, trying to pull burden after burden from my soul. I just wanted it to stop. I didn't want to do this in front of her. I didn't want to air my dirty laundry before her. She was not safe. Finally she said, "Can you get out any more?"

She kept asking horrible questions that I didn't want to answer ...

"I can't find anything," I said.

"Okay, now look at this pile that you've pulled from your body," she instructed. "What does it look like?"

"It's a big tangle at my feet," I said, "It looks kind of like a bush."

"How big is it?" she asked.

"It comes up to my waist," I answered, "but it's really wide, maybe four feet."

"Okay," she said, "You see this big bush of burdens at your feet. The Savior is willing to get rid of this. How does He do it? What happens to it?"

"I don't know," I said. "I think He waves his hand and it begins to fade until it disappears."

"What does He do next?" she asked.

The picture in my head was unclear. I could tell that the Savior wanted to leave, but obviously Suzanne was expecting Him to do more. What was He supposed to do?

"Um," I said. "He calls me by name and invites me to come again if I want to get rid of some more."

"Is there anything else?" she asked. "Does He say anything to you?"

"No," I said. "He left."

"Okay," she said, "You can open your eyes now." She handed me a tissue to wipe my tears.

"Well, you did better than I did my first time," she said. "He called you by name. That's really good."

Actually, I had been working on that one for weeks in my daily declarations. I had been repeating "I am a child of God. He knows my name and He loves me" every day trying to convince myself that it was true. It was reassuring to hear that it had been difficult for her, as well, but I probably didn't really do better than she had, because I kept so much of what I saw hidden and tried to say the parts that I thought she wanted to hear.

> I think the Savior has more that He wants to say to you.

"You're going to have to do this again," she said. "I think the Savior has more that He wants to say to you. I think He wants to tell you that He loves you and tell you how wonderful and amazing you are."

My heart sank. I didn't ever want to do that again. It was awful. It was also incredibly disturbing. Why was I able to be at peace when I was by myself, but as soon as another person was added to the picture, I immediately assumed that I was in danger and I needed to defend myself from an attack? Is that the way I viewed everybody else, as threats to my personal safety? I knew it wasn't always like that. Even more disturbing was the evidence that

I was more comfortable with the image of defending myself from attack, than I was with meeting with the Savior and having Him be willing to accept my burdens. The first scenario was far more believable and I knew what to expect. The second was awkward and unrealistic. Why would the Savior bother to meet one on one with me? I was a nobody.

"I don't think I'll be able to," I pleaded. "I'm going to cry and I hate crying. It's not pretty when I cry. My eyes get red and swollen and it takes two days for the swelling to go down. I get a headache. I hate people asking me if I'm okay. I hate everything about crying."

I hate people asking me if I'm okay. I hate everything about crying.

"Crying is healing," she said. "It's actually one of the fastest ways to release the garbage from inside you. Tears are filled with emotion. They're a great way to release those emotions that have been trapped inside of you."

"I hate it," I repeated.

"Maybe you can find a time when nobody else is home, and you're by yourself. Then you can have time to get composed before you have to face people again," she suggested.

"I'm not going to have any time by myself," I said. "We're going on a family vacation. We have a week at a condo in Eden by Pineview reservoir the same time every year. Unfortunately there's a lot of other stuff going on at the same time and this year hardly anybody is going to be able to come. It will mostly be just me and Lewis."

She raised her eyebrows slightly. "And how is that going to go?" she asked.

"Well," I said, "he's really excited about it and has been talking about all the things we can do with just the two of us."

"I see," she said, "So your plan is to do everything he wants to do and pretend to be happy so he'll have a good time. Am I right?"

"Well, actually, yes," I replied, ashamed by her brutally accurate deduction.

"Let's talk about the teeter-totter again," she said. "Remember the need to give and receive. You're not supposed to be the sacrificial lamb who does everything for everybody else all the time. You are not supposed to be a martyr and you are not just Lewis' sidekick. You are a person. You have needs, too, and you have a right to have those needs met. You will be a better wife if your needs are met."

I wasn't sure how to respond to that, so I didn't say anything.

"Lewis is air energy type, right?" she asked.

"Yes," I said.

"And you're water?" she asked.

"Yes," I replied again.

"We all need to have fun, but fun looks different for different people," she went on. "For Lewis fun means playing, but for you fun is probably to spend time alone to rejuvenate. Am I right?"

"Yes," I answered.

"Is there any way that you can rearrange your vacation so that you can spend some time alone?" she asked. "I am re-energized by being alone where I'm able to think and not worry about taking care of everybody else. I spent a few days away myself to be able to create that women's retreat. Could you do that?"

The very idea startled me.

"I think that would really hurt Lewis' feelings," I said. "He's been looking forward to it."

"Yes, but it's draining the life out of you, isn't it?" she said.

"Well, yes," I said and began to seriously ponder the idea.

"I just saw a flicker of a smile," she said, "The idea really appeals to you doesn't it?"

"Yes," I admitted, "but how could I ever do that?"

"You'll have to talk with Lewis," she said. She gave a few suggestions on how I could approach the topic in a way that wouldn't be offensive.

"Will you do it?" She asked. "Will you ask for time to be alone?"

"Okay," I said. "I'll do it."

"When does your trip begin?" She asked.

"On Saturday," I replied.

"This Saturday, as in three days from now?" She clarified.

"Yes," I replied.

"Okay, will you text me by Friday at noon with his answer?" She asked.

"Okay," I said with a sigh of resignation.

"Good," she nodded. "Let's talk about your homework assignment for the week. I want you to write a letter to God and also write His answer to you," she instructed.

I immediately thought about the movie *Collateral Beauty* and Will Smith's letters to love, time, and death. How on earth do you write a letter to God and how does He write back?

"First to prepare yourself I want you to write the answers to three questions," she began. "The first question is 'What are my thoughts about myself and my relationship to God,' the second is 'What are my thoughts about God?,' and the third is 'What are my thoughts about what God thinks of me?'"

I remembered those questions from the women's retreat and I remembered not wanting to answer them.

"These questions help you determine where you're at. The next part is to help you get where you want to be. When you know what you want to say, write your letter to God. Pour out all the stuff that's bothering you. Dump out all your heartache and tell

Him how you feel. It's okay to vent everything. This is done with the intent to heal and it won't offend Him. You're not just ranting. Anybody can rant and yell at God and it doesn't do anything except make you angrier. This is about healing and getting answers."

"Express your needs," she said. "Then put your pen on the paper and write His response. It's like when you wrote a letter to your body at the retreat. You write a letter and then you write the response. Do you remember doing that?"

"Well, I never actually finished that," I admitted. "I wrote a letter to my body, but I didn't write a response."

"Then you're only doing half," she chided.

Actually, I wasn't doing it at all nor did I have any intention of doing it in the future. Not only did that seem really weird, but I didn't see the point of the exercise.

"Do you understand what you're supposed to be doing?" she asked.

"I don't really think so," I admitted. "It's something about writing until you can't think of anything else to write, but what else? How is this different from the journaling and finding ping pong balls and tearing it up?"

"Okay," she explained. "These are completely different. They are both written, but they have different objectives. When you're 'taking out the trash', you are writing for the purpose of finding the root of the problem so you can get rid of it. That's where you write until you can't think of anything else to say, and then tell your body, 'thanks that was awesome, now dig deeper.' When you're done you tear it up or burn it."

Suzanne continued, "What I'm talking about now is searching for answers to questions. When you're writing this letter to God, do it with a question in your mind. Something like, 'What do you really think about women?', since that is one of the things that's bothering you. Vent all your frustrations and when it's all on the paper, pause and lift the pen to the next line and write, 'Dear Linda.' Wait until the thoughts come to your mind and just write everything. Then read what you've written. This will be your answer. You will discover truth that has been hidden inside you but that you've forgotten. This is done with the intent to heal. I'm assuming you desire to heal, to find truth, and to improve your relationship with God. That's what this is all about. Is that something you want?"

"Well, yes," I said.

"This is kind of like a prayer journal," she explained further. "Sometimes when we pray verbally we say the words out of habit and don't really pay attention. When you're praying with writing you're forced to focus and it amplifies your ability to get answers."

"Okay," I said. "That seems reasonable. I could try that."

"It may also help to find a sacred, peaceful place to do this," she added.

A PATTERN?

She paused to look at her watch, "Well, we've gone over time with the mentoring segment of our time together, so we don't have much time for Body Code, but at least we can address one or two things. What would you like to work on?"

"Oh, just whatever my body needs the most, I guess," I said.

"All right," Suzanne began. "It looks like we need to address another mental image. This one is 'I am a nobody,' and is from around age 25, but we need to know more before we can release it. What was happening in your life about that time?"

"Let's see," I pondered. "That was about the time that Lewis got hired with the airlines. It was also the time his first book was published."

Suzanne paused and looked at me, "And did you edit his book, as well?"

"Yes," I said.

"And is your name on the cover?" she asked.

"No," I said.

She gave me a knowing look as if to say, "Are you recognizing a pattern yet?"

I remembered that exciting yet stressful time when McGraw-Hill accepted Lewis' proposal for a technical book on flying. In his subsequent books, he didn't need my help very much, and nowadays when he writes for various flying magazines I often don't even see the article until after it's been submitted to the editor. However, in that first book the challenge to find the right words to express the desired meaning was painstakingly difficult. I worked with him scrutinizing and revising every word on every page until it was good enough for publication. The project took several months, but it was so satisfying.

Lewis shared the completed manuscript with a former high school friend named Joe who read it and wrote a brief note in response.

"Do you think I should add Joe's name to the book?" Lewis asked one day. "He's an English major and it might look good on his resume to say that he edited a book."

My jaw dropped to the floor. Joe had skimmed through the manuscript once and wrote two sentences with suggestions, yet Lewis wanted to add his name to the cover. I had worked side by side with him for months pouring over every word and every phrase and helped in the selection of photos and captions and ensured that everything was completed in accordance with the contract guidelines and expectations. The unfairness of the suggestion cut me to the core. I talked Lewis out of adding Joe's name to the book. I could handle not getting credit, but giving the credit to Joe was more than I could bear.

"We all need to feel recognized and appreciated for what we do," Suzanne said pulling me out of my reverie. "Remember when I said that I did the Body Code for free for a year? It was awful. No one appreciated my efforts. It wasn't about money. I didn't care that I wasn't getting paid. I was serving out of love, but those I worked with rarely got back with me to let me know it helped or that they appreciated it. I was giving my all and getting nothing back to show it was of any worth to them. It wasn't until I started charging for my services that people valued it. Now my clients always thank me, and I know I'm doing good because people tell me so."

At the conclusion of the agonizing session she hugged me and said, "Linda, you are awesome. I can't wait until you can see it."

I was relieved that it was finally time for me to go home. *Suzanne is not safe*, I thought. *I'm supposed to send her constant updates; some daily, others weekly, and detailed questionnaires before each mentoring session. I never expected that she'd actually read them and ask me about them. She knows too much. I don't want to send any more. I don't want to be weighed and measured by what I do. I plan to only include the most generic 'successes' possible from now on so she can't ask horrible questions. I need to protect myself from her prying eyes. How can I hide from her and still allow her to help me? If I have to choose between the two, I prefer hiding.*

I felt angry, confused, and ashamed. I wanted to quit every bit as much as I did on the very first day. My head was swimming with things that were bothering me. One was the thought of this journal that I've been writing. I felt compelled to do it and to share it, but I never, ever intended to put my name on it.

> My head was swimming with things that were bothering me.

If I have to share, then fine, I'll share because there's a chance it might help another person, I thought, *but no one will ever know who I really am.*

I had created a fictitious name, Lucy Birch, and that is how I planned to publish it, in whatever form it got published. I planned to stay hidden behind the safety of this straw man (woman) and false persona, but all of Suzanne's comments about me writing and never getting the credit were like slaps in the face.

But this is different, I mentally protested. *I need to stay hidden to protect myself. This is not about success and glory; it's about an agonizing and embarrassing struggle for healing. I will be exposed and vulnerable to anybody. There is no way God or anyone else would actually expect me to do this. It's too hard. It's too awful to even think about.*

But I did think about it. I agonized over it for the rest of the day. My daughter noticed my heavy countenance and asked, "Was someone mean to you?"

"No, it's just that..." I began and then changed my mind and said, "Yes. Your Aunt Suzanne was mean to me. She makes me do things I don't want to do. She makes me see myself in new and horrible ways and it's super painful. She makes me face things I want to ignore. She is mean."

My daughter laughed, "You can do this Mom," she assured me.

GOODBYE, LUCY

The wrestling match taking place inside my mind was exhausting. I had never put it into words, but I realized that I assumed that my journey to healing would be to learn how to forgive and let go of my anger so I could be at peace with being walked on and passed over my entire life. I never figured that healing would include learning how to take and receive. This was far more scary than the "happy doormat" scenario that I had unwittingly imagined.

This uncomfortable idea of give and take reminded me of a Mark Gungor video that I saw. Mark Gungor is a sought-after international speaker on marriage and family. His comedic approach makes his youtube videos delightful to watch. I especially enjoyed his hilarious video where he explains the difference between men's brains and women's brains. I remembered in one of his videos that he talked about the natural tendency for women to give and the natural tendency for men to take. The result can be great for the men, and not so great for the women as they wear themselves out. I remembered how he talked about the need for women to learn how to take and how difficult it is for many women to do that. When I watched the program, I didn't think that applied to me, but now that I saw things in a new light; I guess that advice applies to me, after all.

I had sometimes felt resentful about the unfairness of a mostly unidirectional flow of service; now I was being told that it was my fault, or at least partly my fault. I was tired of everything being my fault.

I felt relieved when it was finally time to go to bed and put an end to this distressful day. When morning came and it was time for my morning routine of declarations, shield, and song, I dragged myself to the mirror and forced myself to get through them, but they were uttered in a bland emotionless monotone. I realized that for a while now, I had been doing them for my imaginary friend and alter ego, Lucy. She was the one who could be loved and valued and important. She was the one I had been writing about. I was beginning to believe the declarations "My words have value," and "I have the courage to speak my truth," but I was really talking about Lucy's words, not mine. She could be healed and she could make a difference for good. Did I really have to let her go? My confidence drained to the floor.

I decided to submit my question to the "scripture instant messaging" experiment. I opened the scripture app and used the bookmark tool to find the place where I'd finished reading the day before. In the notebook tool I wrote, "Do you really expect me to expose myself by giving up my pen name and using my own name?"

I began to read hoping that there wouldn't be anything that applied to me and I could dismiss the terrible thought. I didn't know that there were verses of scripture that talk specifically about the importance of names, but apparently there are.

As I re-read the notes that I had written after completing the chapter, I felt a weight of responsibility which pressed unwelcome tears from my eyes. I went to the computer and searched for all the places where I had written the name Lucy and replaced them with my own name. I spent the day in mourning for the demise of my beloved shield and the death of my cherished anonymity.

With a heavy heart, I put on my game face for the day and realized that I still needed to talk to Lewis about the possibility of spending time alone for part of our vacation. Fortunately the condo was only about an hour's drive from our house, so we could be flexible and people could come and go as needed.

"Last year we were really lucky with our week at the condo," I began. "We were able to get everybody together and make a lot of great memories. This year It's going to be really different since some kids can only come part of the time and others won't be able to come at all. Can we break it up into sections? Part of the time can be all of us that are able to come, part of it can be just the two of us, and can I have a couple days just by myself to rejuvenate?"

"You want to go by yourself?!" He cried, taken aback. "Uh, okay. Do you want the whole week alone?"

"No," I replied. "I don't think I need a whole week, but I would like a couple days. Are you okay with that?"

"All right," he said, "Let's figure out the schedule of when everyone is available and make a plan."

I would get two days by myself at the condo. One day would be dedicated to doing my horrible homework assignment from Suzanne and the second day would be to recover so that I could be ready to play with my family when they returned. I wasn't looking forward to this, but I hoped it would be a good thing.

The first two days of vacation were spent playing together as a family and I didn't even need to pretend to be happy since I was genuinely having a good time. One of the activities was going to "ninja gym" which is what my son calls the open gym time at a certain gymnastics school. He wanted the whole family to come and support him as he tried out his tricks of flips, back handsprings, and parkour on the cushioned floor of the gym. We made sure to take lots of pictures and give lots of praise. Afterwards my son repeatedly thanked us for going there with him.

I wasn't looking forward to this, but I hoped it would be a good thing.

"That means a lot to me," he said. "It's no fun to work on tricks with no one to watch."

As I thought about how much it meant to him, I felt the assurance of how important it is to do things that other people want to do even if you don't want to do them. That's part of being a family and supporting each other. So how did that fit in with the idea that I was not a sidekick that had to do everything that everybody else wants? I would always have to do things that I wasn't interested in to support other people. If I only did what I wanted to do, I would be a selfish jerk. There must be a balance somewhere, but I didn't know what that was yet.

THE ASSIGNMENT

The time came for my family to leave me behind as they headed back home. It felt a bit strange. After they left, I stayed up late. I didn't want to go to bed because that meant that when I woke up it would be time to try to write my letter to God and I knew it would be awful and include dreaded tears.

In the morning I completed my morning routine. I added a new song to my list. It's called "Fight Song" by Rachel Platten, and although not all the words fit, there is a line that reminds me of how it feels to do a complete conversation.

And all those things I didn't say
Wrecking balls inside my brain
I will scream them loud tonight
Can you hear my voice this time?

This is my fight song
Take back my life song
Prove I'm alright song

My power's turned on
Starting right now I'll be strong
I'll play my fight song
And I don't really care if nobody else believes
'Cause I've still got a lot of fight left in me

After trying to build myself up with declarations, songs, shield, scriptures, and prayer, I added one more thing. I decided to fast today. There's a scripture in Isaiah 58: 5-11 that explains the benefits of fasting. It talks about how fasting is intended to lighten heavy burdens, and to let the oppressed go free. It also promises that when we fast the Lord hears our cries and answers. It continues with additional beautiful promises of light, healing, and guidance. It embodies all that I hoped to receive.

I went for a long walk in the cool of the morning and enjoyed the beauties of the natural surroundings while trying to decide where I should go to write my letter. The lake would be crowded with people, so the obvious choice was to find a quiet place in the mountains. I searched until I found a secluded camp site with a picnic table where I could sit and write. A small stream with a cascading waterfall flowed nearby and lush vegetation surrounded me.

I wrote out the three questions and filled several pages with my answers. As I wrote it brought a few memories to mind and I paused to have complete conversations with several individuals. Finally I decided it was time to begin the actual letter to God. I wrote and wrote until I couldn't think of anything else to say, then I turned to a new page and wrote "Dear Linda," and waited for thoughts to come into my mind so I could write them down. My mind was a complete blank.

After several moments of still silence I broke down and began to sob. *God has nothing to say to me. I am a fool for ever thinking that He might.*

I tried a new approach and wondered if I could re-enter the previous visualization at Suzanne's house where Christ came to offer to take my burdens. Perhaps if He helped me then Heavenly Father would be willing to address me. My current actual surroundings were similar to the ones I had imagined and I thought that might help, but try as I might, I could not visualize Christ entering the clearing. He simply refused to come.

The entire experiment was an epic failure. My efforts did not result in healing or enlightenment, only puffy red eyes and a headache. I gathered my notebooks and pens from the picnic table and headed dejectedly back to the car for the drive back to the condo.

I'm tired. I think I'll take a nap.

Three separate times I picked up the pen and tried to continue the letter, but each time my mind was a complete blank. I shouldn't have bothered asking for time alone up here. It didn't do any good. I consoled myself by watching the epic BBC version of *Pride and Prejudice* with Collin Firth and Jennifer Ehle, so at least something good happened that day.

The next morning I awoke in a deep melancholy. It was the first time in a couple months that I wished to cease existing. I was back to square one. I fasted a second day and tried a new venue. I drove over the mountain to Ogden city to be near the beautiful LDS temple there. I stayed for hours hoping for a spark of enlightenment, but nothing came.

Once again, I would be returning to the condo as a failure. Anger swelled within my soul until it burst. I had my second yelling, swearing complete conversation. It was with God.

After yelling and sobbing and then asking for forgiveness, I sat down once again with my notebook and pen. I wrote another letter to God with the new insight from all the additional frustrations then I turned the page and wrote, "Dear Linda." This time ideas began to flow. I have to say it was rather anticlimactic, after all that effort I think I was expecting a vision or something.

> *I would be returning to the condo as a failure. Anger swelled within my soul until it burst.*

I don't necessarily believe the message yet, but these are the words that I read in my own handwriting: "You are a beloved daughter of God… I love you more than you are capable of understanding… I love my daughters, they bring glory to me and to all creation. Don't worry, it will all turn out okay. In the end you will be satisfied. It will be better than you ever imagined.

Remember what Bernard taught you about women…Hang on a little longer; it's going to be okay. Let go of your anger and choose to be happy. Trust me. Believe in me. It will all be fair in the end… Don't worry any more. Just be concerned about doing good and being good… Don't fight against what you know to be true just because there are things that you don't understand…"

My friend Bernard was brought to my remembrance. He had a glimpse of heaven when he died for a brief period of time and was revived. He sees life from a different perspective than most people. He doesn't share his experiences with many people because they are sacred to him, but my daughters and I have had the privilege of hearing a few stories and they are always so uplifting. He said that heaven was indescribably beautiful and there are vibrant colors that don't even exist here. He also said that of all the beautiful creations the most glorious were the women. He couldn't even describe them.

I liked that part.

OPENING MY HEART

I had made peace with God; now it was time to make peace with my husband. It was our turn to spend some time alone together at the condo. We went to dinner and went swimming and had a great time. I didn't want to ruin the evening since I wasn't sure how he would respond, so I held my tongue for another day. I didn't sleep well since I was so nervous. In the morning, I invited him to go for a walk with me.

"You've been so kind to me lately, it makes me want to trust you, but I'm scared. I haven't felt emotionally safe with you for a long time. If I opened my heart to you, what would you do with it?" I asked.

"I'd treat it like my own," he answered. "What would you do with mine?"

"I'd treat it with respect," I answered. "I would cherish it."

"Tell me what's on your mind," he said.

"Well, I've been working on myself for a while now and at the last session with Suzanne, something happened that really bothered me," I began. I told him about the visualization and how I saw a hooded figure and realized that I view other people as a threat to my safety. I explained that what I was supposed to be seeing was the Savior and how hard it was to change the mental image and that I was surprised that I felt more comfortable with the idea of the hooded figure scenario because that was more familiar and believable. I feel constantly under threat of attack and I must always be on my guard to protect myself.

"Oh," he said. "That's sad. Where do I fit in?"

"I have been more afraid of you than anyone else," I said with a few tears escaping. "I don't want to be afraid of you. I want to be on the same team..."

He listened. He thanked me for opening up to him. We

walked and talked. I felt a wave of peace wash over me. It was healing for both of us. It was beautiful. Perhaps I should have done that a long time ago, but I wasn't healed enough to make the attempt until that day.

NEW ALLIES

I experienced yet another aftershock of my personal earthquake. It was deeply, personally, intimately painful. Nothing had changed, and yet everything was different because I was changing. Life is still going to be hard, but it's also going to be okay. My relationship with God was healing. My relationship with my husband was healing. I was healing. Because the walls in my relationships were dissipating I didn't have to deal with this one alone. My husband was right there to offer comfort and support. I prayed and asked the Savior to take my burden. My two biggest foes had transformed into my greatest allies.

I understand now that I was not expected to hold onto my pain and make it a part of me. I also understand that if I didn't acknowledge it and choose to let it go, it would become a part of me whether that was my intention or not. Furthermore, I understood in a new way that it is only through the grace of God that letting go and healing are possible.

It has been only two months since I began this journey. They have been two incredibly long and difficult months, but the changes have been monumental. I know that I'm not done and there will still be difficult challenges ahead. This may be a lifelong progression, but it's ever so much better than remaining stagnant.

I started on this journey to overcome my crushing blow, but it's also healing my brokenness and I have hope for a bright future and a new and improved me. In my last mentoring session, Suzanne said, "Linda you are awesome. I can't wait until you see it."

I am beginning to believe her.

LEAVING EMERALD CITY

In the book *The Wonderful Wizard of Oz* by L. Frank Baum, there is a scene that has been left out of the various theatrical interpretations. When Dorothy and her friends come to the Emerald City they are admitted through a laboriously detailed process which includes, among other things, getting a new set of clothing and having a pair of glasses locked onto their heads that cannot be removed without a key and must be worn at all times within the city. They marvel at the unique beauty of the city where everything is green including the lovely dress given to Dorothy upon her arrival. They meet with the wizard who sends them on an impossible quest to complete before he will grant them their wishes. The group then must leave Emerald City in order to complete their task and again go through a lengthy process to leave the city. As the last step before exiting the city gates, they have their glasses unlocked and removed. Dorothy marvels that her lovely green dress has suddenly turned white; surely the Emerald City has wonderfully magical powers. The reader recognizes, of course, that the dress had really been white all along and the glasses had green lenses which made everything, regardless of its actual color, appear green.

I have been wearing colored glasses my entire life. I have always seen my own interpretation of myself and of the events that have taken place in my life. I haven't seen things as they really are.

I think most people see the world through a pair of colored glasses, but we don't even have the advantage of the Emerald City where everybody sees only green, because we're all wearing different colored lenses. Two people can go through the exact same event and come away with entirely different interpretations of what happened. It makes communication and getting along with each other extremely challenging. I think that someday, after this life, we'll all have the chance to see ourselves and others without wearing our glasses and I think most of us will be surprised.

I'm trying to unlock my glasses and leave Emerald City so I can see myself and the world in a new light. So far, it has been terrifying, enlightening, and freeing all at the same time.

THE FAKE ENDING

I ran a 5K with my daughters yesterday. I use the word "ran" because that is the standard verbiage associated with races and not because there was a lot of actual running involved.

My brother ran a 100K once. He and his wife find marathons refreshing, especially if they go through beautiful mountain scenery along dirt pathways. I, on the other hand, loathe running and jogging with a fiery passion. I'm not opposed to physical activity. I thoroughly enjoy my daily 10 mile circuit along the Jordan River Parkway on my comfortable recumbent bicycle. I love the sight of ducks swimming along the gently flowing river lined with trees, the sweet smell of the blonde grasses, the sound of the birds, and the feel of the soft breeze as I pedal along. It feeds my soul. It is exercise that doesn't feel like exercising.

Jogging, on the other hand, is exercise that hurts me and I avoid it whenever possible. Prior to yesterday I had participated in exactly two 5K runs and after the second decided that I would never do it again. Therefore I was less than enthusiastic when my daughter suggested that all the ladies in the family participate in an upcoming 5K. My training consisted of jogging for a single mile on a single day which reminded me of all the reasons why I hate jogging, then I went back to riding my bike and hoped that she would forget all about it. She did not.

The morning of the run dawned bright and sunny promising a hot day ahead. My three lovely daughters, one of whom has a two month old baby and suggested this monstrous activity, gathered at my home and we traveled to the starting point together. As we began jogging along with the throngs of other runners, it didn't take very long before I was overcome with nausea and needed to slow to a walk. I was embarrassed, but it was either that or throw up all over the imminent parade route and I didn't think anyone would appreciate that outcome.

I remembered a recent Facebook post by a friend who walked a 5K recently. She observed that it took her 55 minutes to complete the task, whereas the last time she participated in a 5K she jogged and took 45 minutes. "That's only a 10 minute difference," she said, "I am converted to the idea of walking." Remembering her words comforted me. People have walked through these before and they didn't die of shame; I was going to be okay.

After a while I recovered enough to jog along for another section and continued until the nausea once again overcame me. My sweet daughters stayed with me even though they could easily have left me behind. After a while I began calling out mini goals, "Okay, I'm going to start jogging again at that sign and go until I reach that lamp post." We completed the mini task and walked again until I was ready for the next mini task. We continued along in this manner, slowly but surely progressing towards our goal of finishing.

When we finally passed under the decorative metal archway that was obviously the Arc de Triomphe finish line, we gave each other high fives. It was a bit anticlimactic since we were far from the first to finish and there were now people milling about preparing for the upcoming parade, but we didn't mind. I was a little surprised that I didn't see a time clock to show runners the amount of time that it took to complete the run, but it really didn't matter since we clearly weren't racing.

We rested on the cool lawn under the shade of a large tree. We drank our water bottles, and talked of the plans for the rest of the day. After recovering sufficiently, we took a picture to record the event and began the long walk towards the car. My daughter needed to get back to her baby, so we didn't have time to enjoy the parade.

After a short walk we saw a sign that said "3 mile mark."

Wait? What? I thought we were done, didn't we already cross the finish line? Apparently not. How embarrassing. How did we mess that one up? It made me think of one of my favorite bumper stickers. Sometimes you see stickers on cars that say "26.2" to indicate that the owner has run a marathon, but this one said "27.5" with the added explanation, "I got lost." I thought it was very funny, but I never thought anything like that could actually happen. Oh well.

"Okay," I called out, "the next goal is from here to the finish line… if we can find it."

We jogged the last stretch and passed the actual finish line. Our time was 48 minutes. I have no idea what it would have been if we hadn't stopped and practically taken a nap first.

My underprepared body was aching and when I undressed to take a shower I discovered that my socks were bloody and my feet had blisters, but I had a smile on my face and a twinkle in my eye as I limped along. Of the three 5K's I have done, this one was the most enjoyable. I had the support of my family, and the discovery that I could use mini goals to achieve a greater goal helped make the ordeal more manageable. I could do that again, but I should probably buy a different pair of shoes first.

I didn't mean for the run to be a metaphor for my journey, but I couldn't help but notice the similarities. This was something that was very hard for me and I didn't want to do it. Having support really helped and the idea of mini goals encourages me. It's okay if I have to slow down and take a breath; I just need to keep moving forward. The bloody feet and the fake ending also applied. I thought I had arrived after the last epic battles conquering my enmity with God and my husband. I assumed it would be smooth sailing after that, but it's still painful and the challenges keep coming.

I have begun to share this journal with extended family and friends, and it is absolutely terrifying as I peel off my armor and stand metaphorically naked and vulnerable before a crowd.

It's worse than that dream where you show up at school in your underwear. I can't take it back. Once people have seen me for what I really am, I cannot pretend to be anything else.

Although the majority of responses have been overwhelmingly positive, it hasn't been unanimous. I deeply appreciate the comments of those who have said that reading this is helping them see themselves in a new light and is a catalyst for healing. It confirms that this is something I am supposed to be doing and I'm sacrificing myself for a greater good. However the negative comments tear into my soul as they suggest a confirmation of my old beliefs that I should be hiding rather than sharing. I'm going to need to grow some thicker skin.

I am adding another song to my repertoire. It's called "Believer" by Imagine Dragons. I love the words which speak, among other things, of the growth and beauty that come through pain, but it's also so fun to blast out the music and sing along. Imagine Dragons is a master of the pregnant pause, that intake of breath where you know something big is coming next. It's like riding on a roller coaster and coming to the top of the very first hill and it pauses at the top just before you plummet down the track towards the loop de loop. That's how I feel right now as I know that this journal is nearing its completion and it's nearly time to begin sharing with a wider audience. I'm frightened of what will happen next.

Once people have seen me for what I really am, I cannot pretend to be anything else.

Some of the lyrics are as follows:

First things first
I'ma say all the words inside my head
I'm fired up and tired of the way that things have been, oh ooh
The way that things have been, oh ooh

Second don't you tell me what you think that I can be
I'm the one at the sail, I'm the master of my sea, oh ooh
The master of my sea, oh ooh

I was broken from a young age
Taking my soul into the masses
Write down my poems for the few
That looked at me, took to me, shook to me, feeling me

Singing from heart ache from the pain
Take up my message from the veins
Speaking my lesson from the brain
Seeing the beauty through the pain.

You made me a, you made a believer, believer.
You break me down, you build me up, believer, believer
I let the bullets fly, oh let them rain
My luck, my love, my God, they came from pain.
You made me a, you made me a believer, believer

Third things third
Send a prayer to the ones up above
All the hate that you've heard has turned your spirit to a dove, oh
ooh
Your spirit up above, oh ooh

I was choking in the crowd
Living my brain up in the cloud
Falling like ashes to the ground
Hoping my feelings, they would drown

But they never did, ever lived, ebbing and flowing
Inhibited, limited
Till it broke up and it rained down
It rained down, like pain...

I HAVE TO DO IT

In today's Body Code session with Suzanne she addressed some of the new issues to help me get through them so I can carry on. Some of the fresh emotions we needed to address were shame, worthless, depression, taken for granted, shock and indecisiveness. These are my go-to emotions out of habit. It is so hard trying to create a new idea of myself. My misguided subconscious believes these emotions to be true and safe since they are familiar and comfortable, anything else must be a threat to my safety. This reprogramming of my subconscious programs is going to take some time and a lot more effort.

"I know today is a Body Code session and we don't have a lot of time," Suzanne said, "But we need to take a few minutes to do a little more mentoring to help you get through this new phase."

"Okay," I said.

"I also wanted to ask you something," she added. "At our family barbeque yesterday, you left early and didn't say goodbye. Was it because you were feeling uncomfortable and needed to escape?"

Now that I have let her read this journal, she knows the things that I have been hiding and holding back. I will never be able to get by on half truths again. She expects the whole story now.

"Yes, that was part of it," I admitted. "I have sent out my journal to extended family and friends and I know that some people are reading about me, but no one has spoken to me. I feel like the Emperor parading through the streets naked and people are afraid to admit what they see. I am exposed and I'm scared."

"Have people responded to your story at all?" she inquired.

"Yes, I've received some beautiful heart felt letters telling me that my experiences, although different from theirs, resonated with them and are helping them heal from their own situations," I said. "But not all the responses have been positive. One person that I care about wrote a letter which I interpreted to mean 'Don't do this, you're not qualified. Leave it to the experts who know more than you do,' followed with a warning that if I continue then I will hurt people's feelings and cause irreparable damage. It hit every tender nerve. I'm not good enough. I'm not worthy. I should be ashamed and humiliated for trying, and the worst thought of all is that I could hurt people. My greatest desire is to help, not hurt."

"Don't let it get to you," she said, "You have made yourself vulnerable and that's a good thing. You cannot heal until you allow yourself to be vulnerable. However, I need to warn you that there will be little voices inside your head that will try to rip you apart. If you let any of them in through the cracks it will be like blood in the water and the sharks will attack. You will need to work extra hard to build yourself up and don't allow worry to enter your mind. Your subconscious is trying to keep you safe and comfortable, it will try to stop you because it's not safe and you might die, but your subconscious is wrong and it will all be worth it. You know you're doing the right thing, don't you?"

"Yes," I said.

"I need to warn you about something else," Suzanne continued, "It is often the people closest to us who will try to hold us back. They often do it out of love and concern. They are trying to protect you in the same way that the subconscious is trying to protect you. They do it because they are also coming from a place of misguided subconscious programming."

"When I told Mom about the women's retreat that I was planning," she continued, "She said, 'You can't do that! You can't expect women to pay money to stay with you in a condo. They won't come and listen to you teach them. It will never work!' I finally had to stop her by saying, 'It's okay if you don't want to be a part of this, but this is what I am supposed to be doing and I am going to do it.'"

"Oh," I gasped, "I didn't know that. She came over and sounded all excited about it and wanted me to come. I never would have guessed that she responded to you that way."

"Of course you know that Mom joined me wholeheartedly the very next day and she helped me present at the retreat," Suzanne added. "It's just that her first reaction was to 'protect me' from doing something I'd never attempted before. It's like that wall we talked about on our first session that is between us and our goals. What's on the other side is unfamiliar, unpredictable, and therefore seems quite unsafe. She was simply trying to protect her daughter."

"Thank you for holding firm and going forward to do it anyway," I said. "You saved me when I thought there was no hope."

"I now know that my women's retreat was created for you," she said with emotion in her voice, "I didn't know it then. I had no idea why I felt so driven. I only knew that I had to do it."

And so, dear reader, although I'm terrified, I'm sharing this with you anyway. Perhaps it is for you. I don't know; I only know that I have to do it.

Best wishes,
Linda Bjork

EPILOGUE

More time has passed. Not a lot of time according to the calendar, but it feels like a lifetime. As I read through this journal, it is as if I am reading about a stranger.

I am now a different person. I am at peace with myself. I can even honestly say that I love my body. I haven't lost weight or had a miraculous makeover, but I see things differently. If the body and spirit together make the soul, then my body is a necessary companion to fulfill my mission on earth. When I'm done with this body, that means I'm dead. I figured that I should probably make peace with this companion and become allies rather than being constantly at odds. My body does a pretty good job; I think we can be friends.

I am at peace in my relationships. I love my husband. I love my mom. I love my kids. We're all good. Interesting things are happening. As I am healing, my relationships and the people around me are also healing. I always knew that illness could spread, but I did not know that healing could spread. It is beautiful.

One interesting thing that happened as a result of sharing this journal, is that my sister Becky, who has now been married for over forty years, thought to ask her husband a question. Why, when they were first married, had he said that they could only call her parents once a month and visit every two years? The answer was enlightening. He grew up living far away from his grandparents. He had a lifetime of experience with a long distance relationship. Communication in those days was done primarily through writing letters, and since long distance phone calls were expensive, they were only for special occasions like Christmas and Mother's Day. Long distance travel was expensive and difficult, so when he grew up they visited

> *I am at peace in my relationships. ... We're all good.*

his grandparents about every five years. He thought that was normal and the way things were supposed to be done. When he married his lovely bride and knew that she would be far from her parents, he wanted to reassure her that she could still be close to her family. Rather than waiting for special occasions, she could call every month. Rather than waiting five years, he would make sure that she could visit every two years. From his perspective and experience, he was being really thoughtful, caring, and generous. He's a good man. There are no "bad guys" in this story. I wonder how much heartache would be healed if we could clear up all of our misunderstandings.

On that same day, ages ago, that I felt impressed that I needed to record and share this journal, I had a second impression that I needed to start a non-profit charity to help others. I didn't have a clue how to do that, but I did it anyway and "Hope for Healing" was born. Hope for Healing is a non-profit charity dedicated to helping people become their best selves. The only person that we can change is ourselves, but changing ourselves changes everything. Visit our website at hopeforhealingfoundation.org

In conclusion, I want to share one more lesson that I learned. In the past, I craved praise and recognition from others, and yet ironically whenever I received it, I dismissed the compliments as being untrue. I didn't realize I was doing that until Suzanne mentioned something in a mentoring session.

She was explaining that "personal progress is personal," meaning that how I view myself and my contributions is a personal matter. Waiting for other people to dictate and validate our worth doesn't make any sense. When it comes to me and my self-worth, my opinion is really the only opinion that matters. It was as if someone drew up the shades on the windows of my mind and allowed the light to enter.

"Oh," I said, "I'm allowed to be my own cheerleader? I've always looked to other people to tell me that I am of value." I thought for a moment and then added, "And yet, whenever people praise me or give me compliments I always reject them. What a stupid plan. I rely on others to build me up, which may or may not even happen, but even when it does, I reject it? That is a model that could never work, it can only fail. No wonder I was so frustrated." Suzanne smiled at my epiphany.

> *I'm allowed to be my own cheerleader?*

I'm letting go of my hopeless and inherently flawed model of relying on other people for validation, and my peace and confidence are increasing proportionally. Each day as part of my morning routine I repeat, "I am surrounded by the love of God and His acceptance. I am filled with the love of God and His acceptance. My confidence and self-worth come from the love of God and His acceptance." That is my new and improved choice for a source of validation.

That visualization where I met with the Savior and allowed Him to take my burdens, which was once so uncomfortable and awful, is now a daily habit. As I gratefully and willingly give my burdens to the Lord, he heals them and we embrace. Tears run down my cheeks as I both apologize and thank him, "I am so sorry to have added to your burden. I am so sorry to have caused you pain and suffering, and yet I am so grateful that you're willing to take them. Thank you for healing me. Thank you for saving me." To which he daily replies, "You are worth it because I love you."

When I first shared this journal with my daughter-in-law, she directed me to a song in reply. It is by Stars Go Dim and is titled "You Are Loved." I share it as a conclusion and final message to you.

We hide pain in the weirdest places
Broken souls with smiling faces
Fighting for surrender
For now and the after, yeah

Just look around and you'll see that people
Are scared to say how they really feel
Oh, we all need a little honesty
You are loved

If your heart's in a thousand pieces
If you're lost and you're far from reason
Just look up; know you are loved
Just look up; and know you are loved

When it feels like something's missing
If it hurts but you can't find healing
Just look up, know you are loved
Just look up, know you are loved

We're not made to be superheroes
Photo shopped, all size zeroes
A light not expected
But not quite perfected yet

Look up; see the sun is shining
There's hope on a new horizon
Calling you, it's calling
You are loved

It your heart's in a thousand pieces
If you're lost and you're far from reason

Just look up; know you are loved
Just look up; and know you are loved

When it feels like something's missing
If it hurts but you can't find healing
Just look up, know you are loved
Just look up; know you are loved

You, don't have to prove yourself
Don't try to be someone else
You don't have to prove yourself
Don't try to be someone else

You are loved
Just look up; you are loved
Just look up; you are loved…

ACKNOWLEGEMENTS

First of all, the idea of writing this book did not originate with me. If this has been of any benefit to the reader, the real credit goes to God who loves and cares about you enough to persuade me to share.

I want to express my love and appreciation for my mother. She is the perfect mom for me, and has taught me directly and indirectly the lessons that I personally needed to learn.

Artwork is a collaborative effort directed by the author's mother, Gwen Smith, along with the ladies at Suzanne Lindsay's women's retreat, 2017

This book obviously would not be possible without my mentor, sister, and friend Suzanne Lindsay, since I would not have embarked on a healing journey without her guidance. You can visit her website at lifeunblocked.com.

ABOUT THE AUTHOR

Linda Bjork is the founder and executive director of Hope for Healing non-profit charity and owner of Innovative Joy LLC. She has written several books including *You Got This! an action*  *plan to calm fear, anxiety, worry, and stress; 30 Days to Alleviate Depression; 30 Days to a Better Marriage; Pathway to Happiness;* and *Crushed.*

Her podcast, "Linda's Corner," and blog, "Two Good Things," were created to inspire hope, increase joy, and motivate positive change. Linda's personal mission is to empower people to become their best selves. She has earned degrees from Brigham Young University and the University of the State of New York. She lives with her family in Salt Lake City, Utah. Lindabjorkauthor.com

APPENDIX

Questions for Discussion

1 When we have difficult circumstances in our lives, it's natural to search for a "bad guy" to blame for our problems. In this story there are no actual "bad guys," just people doing the best they can to meet their own needs. Have you ever had an experience where you perceived someone as a "bad guy" in your life and later learned to see things from his or her perspective and it changed your perception and understanding of him or her?

2 How is searching for the root of the problem different than searching for someone to blame?

3 What did the author mean by "my reality is validated"? [p.24] What actions do we take or not take to validate our perception of reality?

4 The author talks about how familiarity is comfortable. What kinds of things in our lives might not be good, but we don't seek to change because they are comfortable? [p. 26]

5 The author describes an experience of longing for death to end her pain. [p. 27-28] What influences her decision to carry on? How do our decisions affect other people?

6 How did the author initially respond to the invitation to learn about ways to heal and become happy? [p. 32-34, 44-45] What influenced her to make the decision to attend the women's retreat?

7 How did the author respond to her husband's attempt at intervention? [p. 40-42] If you were in his situation, what might you be feeling? What would you do? What would you want to have happen? Why do people resist when others offer to help?

8 The author describes feeling like a fraud. [p. 44] What do you think made her feel that way? Have you ever experienced similar feelings?

9 The author describes a phone conversation with her sister [p 44-45]. What does he sister say and do that influences the author's decision? How does it affect you when you feel that other people respect and trust your choices? How might that influence your interactions and expectations of others?

10 At the women's retreat, Suzanne used an example of a bank account with a balance of positive deposits and negative withdrawals [p. 50]. How do you feel about your current balance in your physical, spiritual, mental, emotional, and social areas of your life? Which areas could use some improvement?

11 Can you explain the Law of the Vacuum [p. 50] and how it can inhibit our progress and healing? How can we work in harmony with that law to facilitate and enhance healing and progress?

12 Why is it dangerous to say "what's wrong with me?" [p. 51]

13 The author asks herself the question "Which do I want more, to be proactive and heal or to be validated in my misery?" [p. 52] Why is the answer to that question so important? Why is that question hard to answer?

14 Suzanne talks about comfort zones and growth zones [p. 52-53]. Why must we step out of our comfort zones in order to grow?

15 The author talks about as assignment to write a letter to her body [p. 56]. She actually wrote twice. What did she write on her first attempt? What did she write the second time? Which do you think was a more accurate reflection of her true feelings? What can we do to learn to love our bodies?

16 Suzanne taught that our lives need to be centered like clay on a potter's wheel to keep our relationships healthy and balanced [p. 57]. What does being centered look like to you?

17 We often compare ourselves with others to establish our identity [p. 57]. What is the danger with that source? What are some better sources for establishing our identity? What questions did Suzanne suggest to help a person evaluate his or her beliefs about our identity?

18 The author talks about having mixed feelings about trying tools she learned about at the women's retreat [p. 58-59]. Why do you think she had mixed feelings? How do you respond when things don't work as you hoped or expected? Are you willing to try again?

19 Can you describe the Law of the Harvest [p. 61]? What was the author's initial response to learning about the Law of the Harvest and why do you think she responded that way?

20 The book describes different levels of thought: the conscious and the subconscious [p. 62-63, 68]. Can you describe the role of the subconscious and how it builds its programs? What kinds of

faulty programs might your subconscious be running? How can we upgrade those programs?

21 The author realizes that she has lost her voice [p. 64-65]. Why do you think she didn't notice it before and what did she want after she realized that it was missing? How might recognizing a problem be the first step toward healing?

22 What techniques did Erika use to let go of negative emotions? What techniques did she use to add positive energy? [p. 64-66]

23 Suzanne gives step by step instructions on how to do a "complete conversation" [p. 68- 69-71]. Why do you think saying sorry and asking for forgiveness are crucial components to healing?

24 What warning did Suzanne teach through the object lesson of the ping pong balls? [p. 71] Did Linda's journey to healing include any "ping pong balls"? [p. 151-165] How do you think knowing that this is a part of the process affected her actions and results?

25 What do you think Suzanne meant when she said "Your mess is your message"? [p. 72] What experiences have you had that might be a gift to help others?

26 What feelings, emotions, and memories were triggered in the author when Suzanne asked everyone to dance? [p. 73-74] Are there things that you once enjoyed that you no longer do? What might happen if you did more of what you love?

27 Suzanne taught about four energy types: air, water, fire, and earth. [p. 75-79] How might it be helpful to understand that

significant people in your life may have a different energy type than you?

28 Suzanne shared some challenges that often arise in communication [p. 80-82] Why is communication often a problem in relationships? Are there ways to improve communication?

29 How is forgiving like "letting me off the hook"? [p. 81-83] Why do you think it is often so hard to forgive others? What benefit do you think you might you receive by offering forgiveness to others?

30 What does "if you spot it, you got it" mean? [p. 84-85] If we feel critical and annoyed with the people around us what might that be witnessing about ourselves?

31 What tools and laws did Suzanne utilize to help make her dream of creating a women's retreat become a reality? [p. 85-87] What tools and laws might you use to realize your dreams?

32 What metaphors/examples did Jamie use to explain some of the causes of depression and hope for a brighter future? [p. 89-93] How can metaphors and object lessons help us better understand ourselves and our potential?

33 Jamie recommended taking two specific actions each day to move yourself towards your goal [p. 92] What are your goals and desires? What action steps can you take to move yourself towards your goals and desires?

34 What is a distinction between progression and simply being busy? [p. 92] What perceived benefit do we get from being busy?

How can being busy be a detriment to our progression in what is really important in our lives?

35 What was the author's initial response to Suzanne and Jamie's offers for further training and why did she respond that way? [p. 93-96] What made her change her mind? How do our attitude and perceptions affect what we are willing to try?

36 The author describes her initial attempt at a complete conversation [p. 97-100]. With whom would you like to have a complete conversation with and why? How do you think it might benefit you? What kinds of obstacles might prevent a person from wanting to take that step?

37 The author describes her initial attempt at saying declarations or affirmations [p. 100- 101]. How do you think she felt about the experience? Why do you think she believed or disbelieved the things she said about herself? What things do you believe about yourself? Why do you believe those things? What would you like to believe about yourself? Why does it make a difference what you believe about yourself? Do you believe that it is possible to change what you believe about yourself, why or why not? What obstacles might interfere with making those changes?

38 Did you notice a change in the author's perception as Suzanne introduced their mother? [p. 102-103] What do you think enabled that change in perception? How do you perceive the important people in your life? How might it affect our relationships with others if we're willing to accept that there might be more to the story or another way to look at people?

39 How might it be beneficial in relationships to understand that opposite may mean harmonious, compatible, corresponding and complete? [p. 103]

40 Have you had any opposition in your life that helped you progress and become stronger? [p. 103-104] In what ways can experiencing opposition in your life help you appreciate the good things that you have in your life?

41 What changes did you notice in the author from the time of the beginning of the women's retreat to the end? [p. 47-106] What did she do to continue the momentum on the path of healing? What can you do to begin and continue momentum on a path of healing?

42 The author describes her thoughts and feelings about people trying to "fix" her [p. 107- 108]. How might understanding the thoughts and feelings of a struggling person help us in our approach to offering help? What kinds of things worked and why? What kinds of things didn't work and why?

43 What tools and techniques did the author try on her own to continue with the momentum of healing and progression? [p. 108-109] Do you think her efforts were successful? Why or why not?

44 The author expressed feelings of failure and embarrassment because she needed the help of another person [p. 113]. Why do you think she felt that way? Are you willing to receive help from others, why or why not? How might you be benefited by allowing others to help you?

45 At the author's first mentoring appointment, her mentor taught her about the possibility of hitting a wall [p. 114-22]. Did the author hit a wall? How did she get past it? How might it have been different if the author didn't understand that this might happen? What tools can you use to get past your walls?

46 The author's mentor gave her assignments that she felt uncomfortable and awkward doing [p. 114-122]. Why do you think she did that? Was the author benefitted by doing those uncomfortable and awkward assignments? Do you think you might benefit by trying tools and techniques even though they feel uncomfortable and awkward? Are you willing to try?

47 The author says, "I just wanted to give up" [p. 122]. Why do you think she felt that way? Have you ever felt like giving up? How does our response to those feelings affect our lives, our happiness, and our progression?

48 The author describes feeling shame [p. 123]. Why do you think she felt that emotion? Shame is very different from guilt. Guilt is remorse that "I did something bad" whereas shame is a belief that "I am bad." Guilt allows us to separate ourselves from our actions, but with shame we define ourselves by our actions. Can guilt ever serve us in a positive way? Can shame ever serve us in a positive way? How can we let go of feelings of shame?

49 The author's mentor describes a tendency to try to fix everything and make everybody happy [p. 123-124]. Do you think that is a positive attribute or a negative attribute and why? How might it benefit you to trust that other people are capable of making their own decisions about life?

50 The author says, "I can't imagine a reality where I don't feel worthless, unimportant and unlovable" [p. 125]. Why do you think that such a scenario would be frightening? Do you have beliefs, situations, relationships, and/or patterns that, although they might not be good, are familiar and therefore feel "safe"? What can we do to open our minds to other possibilities?

51 The author says, "I failed again today" [p. 125]. Do you feel that her perception was accurate and why? Do you see evidence of progress even though she might not have recognized it? Do you think if you looked at your life through the eyes of another person you might see more than you currently realize? How might enlarging your perspective benefit you?

52 The author struggled with insecurity and comparing herself with others [p. 129-130, 138-139]. What recommendations did her mentor give to overcome those issues? Do you struggle with insecurity and comparing yourself with others? What are you willing to do to overcome those issues?

53 What tools did the author's mentor recommend to help her feel safer? [p. 130-132] What difference does it make in our lives when we feel safe? What makes you feel safe? What can you do to increase your feelings of safety?

54 What did the author's mentor mean by "the fruit doesn't look like the root"? [p. 132] How might it help to identify the roots of our problems? What tools and techniques can we use to discover the roots of our problems?

55 The author's mentor promised her that people would treat her differently as she changed [p. 133]. How do you think the way we

feel about ourselves affects how other people treat us?

56 Why do you think the author respond by saying, "I could never say that, it's not true" [p. 133-136]. Can you explain how our subconscious affects our belief system? Can you explain tools and techniques to get past the reticular activating system (RAS)?

57 Can you explain how different pathways of thought are like roads? [p. 136] Which thought processes in your mind are like well-traveled highways? Would it benefit you to create new roads?

58 The author was baffled by the discovery that she was feeling both worthless and prideful [p. 138-139]. Why do you think she had those conflicting feelings? Do you think there a better way to meet our needs?

59 The author talks about trying to reconnect with service again [p. 141-143]. How does serving others help us?

60 What evidence do you notice that things are beginning to improve and change? [p. 140- 144]

61 Humiliation, unworthiness, invisibility and worthlessness were the longstanding blueprint for the author's identity [p. 146-148]. How does our blueprint affect what we think about ourselves? What is your blueprint for your identity? What tools and techniques can we use to create a new blueprint for our identity?

62 What excuses did the author use to justify not doing the things she didn't want to do? [p. 149-150] What excuses do you use to justify not doing the things you don't want to do?

63 What tools and techniques did the author use to uncover some of the roots of her problems and let them go? [p. 151-165] Was a single tool sufficient or did it require multiple tools?

64 The author asks herself a question, "Did I want to heal or did I want to be validated in my anger?" [p. 164] Why is the answer to this question so important? Why do you think letting go is a necessary part of healing? What things make it difficult to let go?

65 How does anger provide a false sense of power and justice? [p. 164-165] How can letting go of anger serve us?

66 Even after experiencing much success and progress, the author hit another wall and wanted to give up [p. 166-170]. Why do you think she felt that way? Why do you think it's important to keep going in spite of setbacks?

67 The author's mentor talked about the principle of giving and receiving [p. 168-170]. How does that differ from the author's expectation of the "happy doormat" scenario? [p. 184] Why do you think it is important to learn how to receive? What beliefs make us resistant to receiving?

68 Can you describe what happened when the author tried to visualize a meeting with her higher power? [p. 171-175] Why do you think she responded the way she did?

69 Can you describe the different perceptions about crying that the author and her mentor shared? [p. 175] How do you feel about crying?

70 The author tells her daughter, "Your Aunt Suzanne was mean to me…" [p. 182-183] Why do you think she was feeling that way? Do you think Suzanne was being mean or was she being helpful? How do you feel when someone asks you to do something that is hard for you?

71 The author says, "I was tired of everything being my fault" [p. 184]. Why do you think she felt that way? Why is it both frightening and empowering to understand your role in the creation of and solution to your problems?

72 Why did the author plan to use a pen name for her book? [p. 184-185] How might it be a benefit to herself and to others to claim her own experiences?

73 The author's first attempt to complete her assignment to write a letter to God and write down his answer did not go as she hoped [p. 188-191]. What did she do differently that helped her be able to receive? Why do you think that helped?

74 The author braved sharing her heart with her husband [p. 192-193]. Why do you think that was so difficult for her? How do you think this sharing might affect their relationship? Is there a relationship in your life that would benefit by increased trust and sharing?

75 The author talks about two different states of being which she calls "broken" and "crushed," and later mentions that she started on her journey to overcome her crushing blow, but it also healed her brokenness [p. 194]. What does "broken" look like? What does

it feel like? Is there anything about brokenness that can provide a positive benefit? What does "crushed" look like? What does it feel like? Is there any aspect of being crushed that provides a positive benefit?

76 The author's mentor says, "… you are awesome. I can't wait until you see it." [p. 181, 194] What do you think the significance is of the author saying, "I am beginning to believe her"? Why do you think would that make a difference? Do you believe that you are awesome? What difference would it make in your life if you believed that?

77 Can you describe the analogy of leaving Emerald City? [p. 195-196] How is it helpful to recognize that we may not always see things as they really are? How is it helpful to recognize that others may not always see things as they really are?

78 Can you describe the significance of the analogy of the "fake ending"? [p. 197-202] How is it helpful to realize that there isn't an "ending" but that life is a continual progression?

79 How do you feel about the author's statement, "Once people have seen me for what I really am, I cannot pretend to be anything else" [p. 200]. Do you think it takes courage to allow people to see you as you really are? What do you think are the benefits of allowing people to see you as you really are?

80 What were some of the negative consequences that the author experienced because she shared her story with others? [p. 203-205] Why is it so scary to make ourselves vulnerable? What benefits are there to allowing ourselves to be vulnerable? How can we continue to feel safe when we are authentic and therefore vulnerable?

81 Why do you think the people closest to us are often the ones who try to hold us back? [p. 204-205]

82 How was the author benefited by her mentor's determination to go forward and do what she felt inspired and driven to do? [p. 205] How have you benefited by the author's determination to go forward and do what she felt inspired and driven to do? How might you benefit others by going forward and doing what you have been inspired and driven to do?

83 The author ends the book in an unconventional way; she signs it with her name like the closing of a letter [p. 205]. Why do you think she did it that way? What significance might that have to her and to you?

84 In the epilogue the author says, "As I read through this journal, it is as if I am reading about a stranger" [epilogue]. Why do you think she might feel that way?

85 The author says, "I always knew that illness could spread, but I did not know that healing could spread" [epilogue]. Who do you think might benefit from your healing and progression?

86 At the beginning of the book, the author shared a story about how events relating to her older sister's marriage affected her life [p 23]. In the epilogue she learned additional information explaining more of the "why's" behind the actions. How does understanding 'why' affect how we feel about things? How much time passed before Becky learned why? How did she learn why?

87 The author says, "I didn't have a clue how to do that, but I did it anyway." [epilogue] What things might you be capable of doing,

that you don't currently know how to do? Who might be benefited if you move forward?

88 What is the danger of craving praise and recognition from others as a source of value and self-worth? [epilogue] Why doesn't it work? What might be a better source of validation?

89 What is the message in the song "You Are Loved" by Stars Go Dim? [epilogue] Why do you think the author shares this song as her concluding message?

90 At what point do you think the author had worth and deserved love? At what point do you think she believed she had worth and deserved love? What difference does is make when we believe that we have worth and deserve love?

References

"Believer." Imagine Dragons. Evolve. 2017

"Brave." Sarah Bareilles. The Blessed Unrest. 2013

"Fight song." Rachel Platten. Fight Song. 2015

In Praise of Stay-at-Home Moms. Dr. Laura Schlessinger. 2010 www. drlaura.com

"The Mother Hood." Similac. 2015. https://similac.com/why'similac/ sisterhood-of-motherhood

"Try Everything." Shakira. Zootopia (Original Motion Picture Soundtrack. 2016.

"You Are Loved." Stars Go Dim. Stars Go Dim. 2015

33117461R00127